NEHEMIAH
GAME CHANGER

Innes M. Howe

INNES M. HOWE

Copyright © 2021 Innes M Howe

All rights reserved.

ISBN: 978-7777262-0-1

Scripture quotations, unless otherwise identified, are taken from THE HOLY BIBLE, NEW INTERNATIONAL VERSION®, NIV® Copyright © 1973, 1978, 1984, 2011 by Biblica, Inc.® Used by permission. All rights reserved worldwide.

DEDICATION

I dedicate this book to my grand nieces and nephews and future generations. Several of you have already demonstrated you are Game Changers and others are in training. There is a seed of greatness in each of you. I encourage you to make Jesus Christ the center of your lives and confidently go forward each day to fulfill your destiny while changing your world for the better.

ACKNOWLEDGMENTS

I thank the Holy Spirit for inspiring me to see a different perspective about Nehemiah as well as giving me the drive to publish this piece. I am grateful for the opportunity to become a professor at Kingdom Covenant Leadership Institute. This experience became a building block for writing this book. My family, godchildren and dearest friends, I thank you for believing in me; my spiritual children, you have encouraged me on this journey especially during those times when I lost the zeal to even try. I thank each of you.

TABLE OF CONTENTS

Introduction	7
Chapter 1 Who Is A Game Changer?	9
Chapter 2 The Call and Response	22
Chapter 3 Effective Use of Wait Time	37
Chapter 4 The Plan and Execution	57
Chapter 5 A Highly Organized Kick-Off	66
Chapter 6 A Spiritual Journey Through the Gates	75
Chapter 7 Overcoming Obstacles	84
Chapter 8 Conflict Resolution, Resolve and Victory	100
Chapter 9 The Wrap Up	112
Chapter 10 The Qualities and Characteristics of a Game Changer	128
Notes	140
About The Author	142

INTRODUCTION

The nation of Israel had fallen into disrepair spiritually and emotionally. They had lost hope and the stronger among them were taking advantage of the weaker. This condition was reflected in the broken-down wall that surrounded them. Little did they know that God had assigned a young man in Persia to deliver them and rebuild the wall. He was no other than Nehemiah, the son of Hachaliah. Many scholars regard Nehemiah as one of the great leaders of the Old Testament.

As you comb through the chapters of the Book of Nehemiah, you will discover the sovereignty of God as He uses one man – Nehemiah – to take His people out of despair and disgrace. You will see leadership at its best with the necessary attributes to become a Game Changer for God and His people. During his leadership, Nehemiah faced opposition, threats, and intimidation; but he was totally reliant on God. In the end, he won and completed his assignment in record time.

A study of the period in which he lived revealed that Nehemiah's experience is not unique. The strategy, skills and talents he used are still necessary and relevant for today.

You may wake one day and face a world that seems to have shifted on its axis overnight causing everything to go topsy-turvy. In the face of turbulence and uncertainty, I encourage you to be like Nehemiah.

I invite you to join me on this journey and discover how having a heart to serve others can cause you to change, not only the trajectory of your life, but also the lives of others. Nothing can be more rewarding.

You will see how burdened over the condition of his people and their city, one man set out to be used by God to right this wrong and bring Him glory.

God created each of us with an innate ability to lead at different levels and in varied spheres. Learn how you, like Nehemiah, can become a ***Game Changer*** for your family, your workplace, your community, and your world."

Nehemiah did it, so can you!

Innes M. Howe
ONTARIO, CANADA

Chapter 1

WHO IS A GAME CHANGER?

For several years, I have been fascinated with the Bible story about Nehemiah to the point that one of my alias names is "Nehemiah." What captured my heart is the strong relationship between servanthood and leadership found in this great man of God. Why then, would God impress upon me to refer to Nehemiah as the *Game Changer*? The answer to my question could be that God is looking for people with a Nehemiah-mindset and I believe you are reading this book because God is calling you to be a Game Changer.

I pray that by the end of the last chapter, you will either confirm you are a Game Changer, or you will decide to become one. Whatever the case may be, I trust you will hear the still quiet voice of the Holy Spirit say to you, *"Be strong and courageous. Do not be afraid or terrified because of them, for the Lord your God goes with you; he will never leave you nor forsake you."* Deuteronomy 31:6 Today, you will embark on a new journey in life.

Technology has caused the world to become smaller and organizations are looking for a competitive edge to improve their bottom line. They are looking for someone or something to radically change their current position to catapult them to the top of their game. People are looking for leaders with specific qualities that could make a lasting change in their lives. They are looking for Game Changers.

I believe the Church has the answer, and God is beckoning us to examine the leadership of his son Nehemiah so that we may become transformed to transform others.

Who is a Game Changer?

The term Game Changer emerged in the 20th Century; some say in 1993 to be exact.

Simply stated, as the term suggests, a Game Changer changes the game. It could be in sports, the direction of an organization, a family, a city, or a country.

According to the Oxford Advance Learner's Dictionary[1] and Investopedia[2] – a Game Changer is a person, an idea, or an event that completely changes the way a situation develops; has new and different ideas that stand out from the crowd. Companies employ this tactic to create ideas or events that change the outcome of a plan. A visionary strategist uses creative innovation to alter their business plans or conceives an entirely new plan by exploring new locations and different products.

A Game Changer deploys innovative strategies to accomplish the desired goal. This is true in the world of sports when the team is losing a game and the coach calls on designated players to come in at a pivotal time. By using their talents, skills, and abilities, these individuals are able to change the course of the game to lead the team to victory.

From a simple point of view, I would add that a Game Changer is one who sees a need and does something to bring about change. It can also be something introduced to fulfill a need like an invention that improves the way things are done. It could be the development and introduction of a new medicine that prevents negative or catastrophic situations from continuing. In so doing, it changes the course of history. We see these types of changes happening at a rapid pace with the ongoing development of technology.

Let us examine some biblical examples of Game Changers. Many scholars and generals have studied the Bible to develop leadership strategies to bring about impactful changes and win battles. The Old Testament is replete with stories of battles that were fought and won under great leaders such as Moses, Joshua and David to name a few.

I find it ironic that many Christians pay thousands of dollars to attend leadership seminars, outside the Church, to learn from someone, who the world deems to be an expert in leadership, when we have a manual, called the Bible, filled with relevant information on this topic. If only many of us would invest time reading this wonderful book.

In no way am I advocating people should not attend these seminars, for there is always something to be learned. I am bringing to bear that when we analyze many of these leadership strategies and recommendations, they tie back to the experiences of great leaders recorded in the Bible.

As we focus on a Game Changer let us consider the following spiritual examples:

GOD - THE ULTIMATE AND GREATEST GAME CHANGER OF ALL

According to Genesis 1:27 God made us in His image and likeness. Therefore, we would expect that if He is looking for Game Changers, He would first look at His creation. This means we must be a reflection of who He is and believe that each of us can be a Game Changer.

Numerous examples that would lead us to see God as a Game Changer are recorded in the Bible; however, for purposes of this discussion I will cite only one:

The Creation:

Genesis 1:2-5 " [2] Now the earth was formless and empty, darkness was over the surface of the deep, and the Spirit of God was hovering over the waters. [3] And God said, "Let there be light," and there was light. [4] God saw that the light was good, and he separated the light from the darkness. [5] God called the light "day," and the darkness he called "night." And there was evening, and there was morning—the first day."

For six days, God transformed something that was formless and void and brought forth all that mankind would need for survival. In addition, He made mankind (male and female) in His image and likeness. If we could only believe this truth and get to know Him intimately by aspiring to grow like His Son Jesus Christ, our lives would be changed forever.

Notice God used words to command and bring everything into being. I have this image of God saying, "let there be light" and at the sound of His voice every element and particle of light that was hidden in the earth responding from wherever it was and coming together to create light. Amazing! Even the elements knew His voice. We learn in the Bible that God's Son, Jesus, also used His voice to perform miracles including one where He stopped the wind from blowing and causing turbulence (see Mark 4:39).

The thought of any of us using our voice in this manner prompts me to contemplate on these questions – How impactful are your words? Do they have weight? Are they trustworthy? As a leader, can your words cause situations within your sphere of influence to shift?

God demonstrated His **Power, Sovereignty, and Deity** to transform the earth by bringing order to chaos. Once He made man, He gave them the mandate to lead.

Genesis 1:28 God blessed them and said to them, "Be fruitful and increase in number; fill the earth and subdue it. Rule over the fish in the sea and the birds in the sky and over every living creature that moves on the ground"

It is essential to pay special attention to this passage of scripture, which underscores my earlier statement that each of us has the inherent ability to lead. We are made in the image and likeness of God to rule.

Embedded in rulership is the ability to lead. If only we can become keenly aware that when God created us, He breathed His Spirit in us. As a result, a spirit of leadership resides within each of us. This means being a leader is a reflection of God. What is missing then is an attitude that says, I can and will lead.

Now, you may ask, "If everyone is leading, who is following?" We will each lead in our sphere of influence at different times and different levels. Serving is a training ground for leadership. Jesus said whoever wishes to lead must first serve – **Mark 10:42-45**. As we study the Book of Nehemiah, we will see that he served before he led.

Mark 10:42-45 "[42] Jesus called them together and said, "You know that those who are regarded as rulers of the Gentiles lord it over them, and their high officials exercise authority over them. [43] Not so with you. Instead, whoever wants to become great among you must be your servant, [44] and whoever wants to be first must be slave of all. [45] For even the Son of Man did not come to be served, but to serve, and to give his life as ransom for many."

JESUS - THE SON OF GOD

Of course, there are many stories in which Jesus exemplified the characteristics of a Game Changer; however, we will review only one example. In the Garden of Eden, Adam and Eve disobeyed God and plunged the human race into spiritual death for eternity. However, God had a redemptive plan. Through the death on the cross of His Son, Jesus Christ and His resurrection from the grave, He made a way for those who believe in Jesus Christ and receive Him as their Lord and Saviour to have eternal life instead of eternal death. Jesus was Purpose Driven and Obedient. He only did what the Father told Him to do. His act of obedience provided a way for mankind to change their eternal destination forever. This outcome for humanity represents a phenomenal change. Now it is up to each of us to choose – eternal life or eternal death. Here are some scriptures to ponder:

Genesis 3:15 And I will put enmity between you and the woman, and between your offspring and hers; he will crush your head, and you will strike his heel.

John 3:16 For God so loved the world that he gave his one and only Son, that whoever believes in him shall not perish but have eternal life.

1 John 3:8 The one who does what is sinful is of the devil because the devil has been sinning from the beginning. The reason the Son of God appeared was to destroy the devil's work.

MARY – THE MOTHER OF JESUS

In Mary's encounter with the angel, she submitted to the Lordship of God by yielding her body for the purposes of God to be fulfilled. In case you are thinking you are too young to be a Game Changer, Mary was a very young girl when she accepted this responsibility. Her submission to God was immediate once the angel answered her question about how it would be possible for her to become pregnant when she was a virgin. She did not ask the angel to wait while she went and checked with her mother or Joseph. She was obedient to God. In those days, to become pregnant out of wedlock could result in being stoned to death. So, she was also a risk taker who God used to change the course for humanity forever.

Luke 1:26-38 (NKJV) [26] Now in the sixth month the angel Gabriel was sent by God to a city of Galilee named Nazareth, [27] to a virgin betrothed to a man whose name was Joseph, of the house of David. The virgin's name was Mary. [28] And having come in, the angel said to her, "Rejoice, highly favoured one, the Lord is with you; blessed are you among women!" [29] But when she saw him, she was troubled at his saying, and considered what manner of greeting this was. [30] Then the angel said to her, "Do not be afraid, Mary, for you have found favour with God. [31] And behold, you will conceive in your womb and bring forth a Son, and shall call His name Jesus. [32] He will be great, and will be called the Son of the Highest; and the Lord God will give Him the throne of His father David. [33] And He will reign over the house of Jacob forever, and of His kingdom there will be no end." [34] Then Mary said to the angel, "How can this be, since I do not know a man?" [35] And the angel answered and said to her, "The Holy Spirit will come upon you, and the power of the Highest will overshadow you; therefore, also, that Holy One who is to be born will be called the Son of God. [36] Now indeed, Elizabeth your relative has also conceived a son in her old age; and this is now the sixth month for her who was called barren. [37] For with God nothing will be impossible." [38] Then Mary said, "Behold the maidservant of the Lord! Let it be to me according to your word." And the angel departed from her.

APOSTLE PAUL

There are many biblical accounts that would cause Apostle Paul to qualify as a Game Changer. Every place he went and preached the gospel, he created a wave. However, I will only refer to his experience in Philippi and Thessalonica. His teaching about the Messiah created a stir that caused the Jews to drive him and Silas out of their cities. While in Thessalonica the people reported, *"These who have turned the world upside down have come here too."* **Acts 17:6 NKJV**. Although they were driven out of town, they left a remnant of Christians that continued to follow Christ. The Apostle Paul was unstoppable even unto death. He was radical.

Examples of Game Changers in Our Day

History has recorded stories of many Game Changers. In political arenas, we have seen great leaders emerge to change the direction of governments, policies, and nations. Nelson Mandela was one of them. He accomplished many things, and no doubt, the one he will be most remembered for was his fight, sacrifice, and leadership that made the way to end Apartheid practices in South Africa. He also became the first black president in the history of that nation.

In technology and business, many leaders, some better known than others, have changed how we interact and transact business on many fronts. These are Game Changers

In education, we read many stories where teachers take a special interest in students who may be walking down the wrong path of life and help them to believe in themselves. As a result, these students changed their ways and became successful in the end. These teachers are Game Changers, and so are the students.

History is filled with many regular citizens who have taken a stand against injustice personally or as a group. Rosa Parks was known as a civil rights activist. On

December 1, 1955, she decided she had enough of segregation that required her to sit at the back of the bus because of her skin color. Therefore, she took a stand by not following this constraint and changed the course of history for her people by sitting at the front of the bus. As a result of her boldness and conviction, today, people of colour are no longer required to sit at the back of buses in the United States of America.

I trust you have gained a good sense of what the term Game Changer stands for. So, let us look at the life of Nehemiah.

Chapter 2

THE CALL AND RESPONSE

To fully appreciate God's work in someone's life, it is essential to study their background – where they came from; how they were positioned in the overall scheme of things. Nehemiah is no different. So, let us look at history.

During the period of King David's reign, he defeated the neighbouring enemies and expanded Israel's territory tenfold. Just before his death, he made his son Solomon king. While Solomon started his reign strong and wholeheartedly depending on God's guidance, he compromised his integrity by allowing idol worship in Israel in his later years. Such action resulted in God's judgment against his people.

1 Kings 11:11 So the Lord said to Solomon, "since this is your attitude and you have not kept my covenant and my decrees, which I commanded you, I will most certainly tear the kingdom away from you and give it to one of your subordinates."

When Solomon died, the nation's military ranks split and Israel became a divided kingdom. Ten tribes migrated to the north and settled in Samaria, while the other two settled in the south in Jerusalem and surrounding areas. The north was called Israel and the south Judah.

This was a hard blow for God's people. "They reached their darkest hour nationally, not when they were attacked from without; but when they were divided within when the walls of their spiritual heritage began to crumble."[1]

During the years that ensued, the people of both sides turned away from the true and living God of their ancestors and turned to worship false gods. God's wrath came upon them and He allowed the Assyrians to invade and conquer Israel in 722 BC.

In 586 BC, the Babylonian king Nebuchadnezzar, invaded Jerusalem and all of Judah and took the people captive. This marked a brutal end of Judah as recorded in:

2 Chronicles 36:18-19 [18] *He carried to Babylon all the articles from the temple of God, both large and small, and the treasures of the Lord's temple and the treasures of the king and his officials. [19] They set fire to God's temple and broke down the wall of Jerusalem; they burned all the palaces and destroyed everything of value there.*

It is important to note what happened to the temple of God and the wall of Jerusalem, as this will play an important part later in the book.

As long as God's people remained connected to Him, revered, exalted and placed Him first in their lives, they lived in peace.

They started well and now they are taken into captivity by their enemy. I often say to those around me that how we start does not matter as much as how we finish.

God is merciful and kind. After approximately seventy years passed, the Medes and Persians captured Babylon and God used King Cyrus of Persia, who did not believe in Him, to free His people.

2 Chronicles 36:22-23 [22] In the first year of Cyrus king of Persia, in order to fulfill the word of the Lord spoken by Jeremiah, the Lord moved the heart of Cyrus king of Persia to make a proclamation throughout his realm and also to put it in writing: [23] "This is what Cyrus king of Persia says: "'The Lord, the God of heaven, has given me all the kingdoms of the earth, and he has appointed me to build a temple for him at Jerusalem in Judah. Any of his people among you may go up and may the Lord their God be with them.'"

This return home is sometimes referred to as the Second Exodus. The first group to return was led by Zerubbabel, who reconstructed the temple; the second was Ezra, who restored worship, but the wall still laid in ruin. God always has a person for the job.

We may find it unusual that God would use someone who does not believe in Him to lead one of His major projects. However, we must remember that everyone is born with a purpose.

Therefore, when God has a job to be done, He will select the right person, according to His overall plan. He simply moved on King Cyrus' heart to execute His plan. This act confirms **Proverbs 21:1** that states: *"The king's heart is like a stream of water directed by the LORD; he guides it wherever he pleases"*. It also gives us the assurance that God will find the right resources when He assigns a project.

Years later, when Nehemiah returned from exile, he did not return to Jerusalem. He remained in Persia, where he occupied the role of cupbearer to King Artaxerxes.

The name Nehemiah means Jehovah comforts or encourages.

Nehemiah held the esteemed position of cupbearer to the king. In this role, he was required to taste the king's food and wine before serving the king and guard his sleeping quarters. Fulfilling the responsibilities of the job is tantamount to saying, "I would rather die than cause harm to come to you." It is possible that members of the Secret Service who surround a President or Head of State may be called upon to make a similar pledge.

It is likely that Nehemiah's lifestyle, prior to being engaged in this position, was exemplary and outstanding. His honesty and integrity must have been unquestionable to the point where a pagan king felt comfortable having him occupy this key position in the king's court.

"Historians have suggested that the cupbearer typically wielded great political influence, even more, than the king's own family. One Old Testament scholar mentions that the cupbearer was often chosen for his personal beauty and attraction. In ancient oriental courts, he was always a person of rank and importance. From the confidential nature of his duties and his frequent access to the royal presence, he possessed great influence".[2]

Of all the people in Persia, God allowed a Hebrew man to be placed in this position of high office to a foreign king for His purposes.

In the Old Testament, we read of how Daniel, Joseph and Esther experienced God's favour with kings of other nations, which reminds us that God is Sovereign. Wherever we are today, we must acknowledge we are in training for His higher good.

Nehemiah would have ready access to the king in this trusted position and perhaps, on occasion, the king may have shared some of his innermost thoughts with him. After all, he trusted Nehemiah with his life.

I recall that while working with one of Canada's largest financial institutions, I became impressed at how those who served the senior executives by cleaning their shoes, cutting their hair, or serving them meals, were able to have in-depth chats with them about personal matters which was something many senior leaders within the organization did not experience.

A New Day Unfolds

Nehemiah's day may have started like any other day as he went about his routine tasks. Then his brother Hanani and some other Jews visited from Jerusalem. Like most immigrants in a foreign country, when they connect with relatives or anyone from their home country, one of the first questions asked is, "How are things back home?" Somehow, they hope for good news about improvements, a thriving economy and their fellow countrymen doing well. Nehemiah would have been no different.

Nehemiah 1:3-4 [3] *They said to me, "Those who survived the exile and are back in the province are in great trouble and disgrace. The wall of Jerusalem is broken down, and its gates have been burned with fire."* [4] *When I heard these things, I sat down and wept. For some days, I mourned and fasted and prayed before the God of heaven."*

Even though Nehemiah was not born in Jerusalem, he had a strong kinship to the place of his parents' and ancestors' birth. Perhaps his parents followed God's instructions about the Passover, to the extent possible, while in exile and passed on the stories.

Exodus 12:25-27 [25] *When you enter the land that the Lord will give you as he promised, observe this ceremony.* [26] *And when your children ask you, 'What does this ceremony mean to you?'* [27] *then tell them, 'It is the Passover sacrifice to the Lord, who passed over the houses of the Israelites in Egypt and spared our homes when he struck down the Egyptians.'"*

Highlights of the report were:

- God's people were living in trouble and disgrace.
- The walls around them were broken and the gates burnt by fire.
- The enemy had struck them.
- The entry and protection to the city was burnt.
- They were exposed and vulnerable.
- They were left in shame.

Upon hearing this news, something seemed to have tugged at Nehemiah's heart. It may have been a call from God. *"Deep was calling onto deep."* Psalm 42:7. His time to be God's agent had come. He was stirred to bring about a solution for his people and deliver them from this disgraceful situation. After all, they were God's chosen people.

One could imagine the dilemma he faced to make a choice between his job and the call. His heart may have been torn between the job he carried out for years as a cupbearer and the fact that he must leave to obey God's call. He may have also found himself in a predicament as he assessed the risk of approaching the king for permission to leave. In his position as cupbearer in the king's court, he may have been aware that the king had previously issued a letter stopping all work on the building in Jerusalem during Ezra's leadership.

Ezra 4:21-22 [21] *"Now issue an order to these men to stop work, so that this city will not be rebuilt until I so order.* [22] *Be careful not to neglect this matter. Why let this threat grow, to the detriment of the royal interests?"*

Clearly, Nehemiah was a man of action. There is a saying "do not ask about the problem if you do not want to be part of the solution." Nehemiah was stricken with grief at this news so he sat down, wept, mourned, fasted and prayed to God.

Putting First Things First

His first response to this call was to pray a specific prayer. He knew he was called to war and could not succeed without God on his side. Although he was born in exile, it is clear he had a close relationship with God. He did not ponder or worry. He went straight to God. Perhaps he had seen his parents or those amongst God's remnant crying out to God in their times of distress. So, he prayed:

Nehemiah 1:5-11 [5] Then I said: "Lord, the God of heaven, the great and awesome God, who keeps his covenant of love with those who love him and keep his commandments, [6] let your ear be attentive and your eyes open to hear the prayer your servant is praying before you day and night for your servants, the people of Israel. I confess the sins we Israelites, including myself and my father's family, have committed against you. [7] We have acted very wickedly toward you. We have not obeyed the commands, decrees, and laws you gave your servant Moses." [8] "Remember the instruction you gave your servant Moses, saying, 'If you are unfaithful, I will scatter you among the nations, [9] but if you return to me and obey my commands, then even if your exiled people are at the farthest horizon, I will gather them from there and bring them to the place I have chosen as a dwelling for my Name.' [10] *"They are your servants and your people, whom you redeemed by your great strength and your mighty hand.* [11] *Lord, let your ear be attentive to the prayer of this your servant and to the prayer of your servants who delight in revering your name. Give your servant success today by granting him favour in the presence of this man."*

This powerful prayer mirrors the Lord's Prayer to some extent. It demonstrates Nehemiah's humility before God and his trust in God to help him. His mind was made up, and he would move forward to obey God. In his prayer, he:

- Exalted God by acknowledging His Sovereignty.

- Reminded God of His covenant love for His people who are faithful and walk in His ways.

- Pleaded to God for His undivided attention.

- Confessed his sins and those of his father's family and the people of Israel.

- Acknowledged that because they disobeyed God's command, they were sent in exile.

- Reminded God that, in His mercy, He said that if His people return to Him, He will gather them from the farthest horizon (corners of the world) and bring them to His chosen place for His namesake.

- Asked for God's favour when he goes before the king.

The Power of Prayer

- Acknowledges your need for God's help.

- Helps to strengthen your faith.

- Brings peace to your soul once you place God in charge of the situation.

- Helps you to stay focused.

Here are some of the leadership qualities seen in Nehemiah in this Chapter:

1. **Strategic Thinker** - With this mindset, an individual thinks about the team, the family, the organization, the Ministry, the country, the world and not about self. Today we live in a world where corruption in leadership is rampant in government, organizations and sad to say, in Ministries. It reflects a type of leadership that is self-centered. They are all about self rather than the greater need God wants us to see. The report about his fellow Jews at home and their living conditions were not good. Nehemiah could have easily said, "I am so sorry to hear. Perhaps one day, they will get the help they need." After all, he had a very comfortable lifestyle. He held a very important position in Persia; so, why would he want to disrupt his life for the unknown?

2. **Readiness and Availability -** You must be ready and available to move when called for an assignment. This preparedness applies to ministry, the workplace, sports and family or wherever God wishes to use you. Notice Nehemiah did not hesitate to pray to God to determine if He wanted

him to go on this assignment. Like Jesus he was ready to leave everything he had become accustomed to and go to get God's job done.

I continue to be moved by the Virgin Mary's response to God's call on her life to bear and give birth to His son. Although she would have quickly calculated the risk knowing she was single and could be stoned to death, she yielded to God's will in this famous response "may it be unto me according to your will." **Luke 1:38**. She did not say, "let me discuss this situation with my parents first." In the game of football, it is called "the next man up." Each player must be ready at all times as they could be called on at a moment's notice to enter the game.

3. **Trust in God** -He only tasks you with what He has already equipped you to do. Nehemiah must have developed a very close relationship with God and must have been told by his parents and others in exile about the great things God did for his ancestors.

4. **Humility** -Even though Nehemiah did not know the details of the project ahead, he knew he could not undertake such a massive project without money, resources and the favour of the king whom he served. Most of all, like Moses, he would not start this project unless God went with him. He acknowledged he needed help.

5. **Wisdom** - Although Nehemiah worked for a powerful king with whom he had a close relationship and influence; he did not rush to the king with his concern to plead a case on behalf of his people. He went to the God of all gods, King of all kings. He was already aware that the king stopped work on the rebuilding of Jerusalem under Ezra. Therefore, he needed the king's heart to turn towards him with favour.

Chapter 3

EFFECTIVE USE OF WAIT TIME

Four months passed after Nehemiah prayed and fasted before he took any action - from Chislev (November – December) to Nisan (March-April). He must have been waiting for the opportune time, as led by God, to approach the king with his request. He had asked God specifically to give him favour when he approached the king.

Nehemiah 1:11 "Give your servant success today by granting him favour in the presence of this man."

Proverbs 21:1 (NKJV) tells us:

The king's heart is in the hand of the Lord, Like the rivers of water; He turns it wherever He wishes.

When we understand the power God had over King Artaxerxes, who else could Nehemiah have turned to? For him to ask for favour he would have assessed what he needed to make the long trip to Jerusalem a success. Perhaps during those four months of waiting, he completed a needs analysis, drew up a plan with a detailed road map and a list of the required resources. From a corporate standpoint, when undertaking a project of this magnitude, you would develop a plan to be used as a road map to get the job done.

It is quite one thing to go to the boss to gain approval to undertake a project that would benefit the organization and show how successful completion would add to the bottom-line. However, it would not be so palatable to approach the boss to ask permission to undertake a project that would require your taking a leave of absence from work so that your countrymen could benefit, unless you are joining the army.

Nehemiah, however, had prayed to the only true and living God of Heaven and he decided he would undertake this project in obedience to God. Armed with a plan and God on his side, he was ready to approach the king when God presented him with the opportunity to do so.

Permit me to segue to the topic of waiting once we have prayed. Often, after praying and waiting for God to respond and time passes without an answer, many give up and decide to pursue a path based on what they know, only to be short-changed from the best God had for them.

There are serious ramifications to going ahead of God's plan for you. In many cases, this behaviour is often driven by selfish ambition, intolerance, doubt, or short-sightedness. It could cost you your kingdom or birthright, or something precious to you as was the case with individuals in these stories from the Bible:

King Saul lost his kingdom because he could not wait for Samuel to conduct the priestly affairs. Samuel was late in keeping the appointment and the soldiers were getting disgruntled. Without seeking God's counsel, he decided to disobey God's command by offering the sacrifice. No sooner had he done so, Samuel showed up. King Saul would soon learn from Samuel that what he did was foolish and that to obey God is better than sacrifice. This is such a valuable lesson for all of us.

1 Samuel 13: 7-14 [7] Some Hebrews even crossed the Jordan to the land of Gad and Gilead. Saul remained at Gilgal, and all the troops with him were quaking with fear.
[8] He waited seven days, the time set by Samuel; but Samuel did not come to Gilgal, and Saul's men began to scatter.
[9] So he said, "Bring me the burnt offering and the fellowship offerings." And Saul offered up the burnt offering. [10] Just as he finished making the offering, Samuel

arrived, and Saul went out to greet him. [11] *"What have you done?" asked Samuel. Saul replied, "When I saw that the men were scattering, and that you did not come at the set time, and that the Philistines were assembling at Mikmash,* [12] *I thought, 'Now the Philistines will come down against me at Gilgal, and I have not sought the Lord's favor.' So I felt compelled to offer the burnt offering."* [13] *"You have done a foolish thing," Samuel said. "You have not kept the command the Lord your God gave you; if you had, he would have established your kingdom over Israel for all time.* [14] *But now your kingdom will not endure; the Lord has sought out a man after his own heart and appointed him ruler of his people, because you have not kept the Lord's command."*

Sarah thought God was taking too long for her to become pregnant with the promised child. So, she encouraged Abraham to sleep with her handmaiden, which resulted in the birth of Ishmael. When the promised child, Isaac, came along, it caused strife in the family and Hagar and Ishmael had to be sent away.

Genesis 6:2-4 Now Sarai, Abram's wife, had borne him no children. But she had an Egyptian slave named Hagar; [2] *so she said to Abram, "The Lord has kept me from having children. Go, sleep with my slave; perhaps I can build a family through her." Abram agreed to what Sarai said.* [3] *So after Abram had been living in Canaan ten years, Sarai his wife took her Egyptian slave Hagar and gave her to her husband to be his wife.* [4] *He slept with Hagar, and she conceived.*

Genesis 21:8-14 [8] *The child grew and was weaned, and on the day Isaac was weaned Abraham held a great feast.* [9] *But Sarah saw that the son whom Hagar the Egyptian had borne to Abraham was mocking,* [10] *and she said to Abraham, "Get rid of that slave woman and her son, for that woman's son will never share in the inheritance with my son Isaac."* [11] *The matter distressed Abraham greatly because it concerned his son.* [12] *But God said to him, "Do not be so distressed about the boy and your slave woman. Listen to whatever Sarah tells you, because it is through Isaac that your offspring will be reckoned.* [13] *I will make the son of the slave into a nation also, because he is your offspring."* [14] *Early the next morning Abraham took some food and a skin of water and gave them to Hagar. He set them on her shoulders and then sent her off with the boy. She went on her way and wandered in the Desert of Beersheba.*

Esau became so hungry after he had been out hunting that he sold his birthright to his crafty brother Jacob and lost his blessings as Isaac's firstborn son.

Genesis 25:29-34 [29] *Once when Jacob was cooking some stew, Esau came in from the open country, famished.* [30] *He said to Jacob, "Quick, let me have some of that red stew! I'm famished!" (That is why he was also called Edom.)* [31] *Jacob replied, "First sell me your birthright."* [32] *"Look, I am about to die," Esau said. "What good is the birthright to me?"* [33] *But Jacob said, "Swear to me first." So he swore an oath to him, selling his birthright to Jacob.* [34] *Then Jacob gave Esau some bread and some lentil stew. He ate and drank, and then got up and left. So, Esau despised his birthright."*

Isaiah 40:31 (KJV) "But they that wait upon the LORD shall renew their strength; they shall mount up with wings as eagles; they shall run, and not be weary; and they shall walk, and not faint."

The word *wait* does not mean to stop all activities. No, it is an action word. The Hebrew Word "qawa" means to hope for or look out for. Notice the word "hope" the mother of Faith – "the substance of things hoped for and the evidence of things not seen." Hebrews 11:1

The result of waiting:

1. Renewed strength – Hebrew "halap" means: pass on; sweep by; to be new; to pierce; cut through; to change, strike through.

2. Mount up with wings like an eagle – Hebrew "ala" is a loaded word – means lift up; come up; to be elevated; to be exalted; cause you to ascend; increase; restore; perfected; excel; shoot up.

3. Run and not be weary – Hebrew "rus" means: to hurry; be a messenger; chase; brought hastily.

4. Walk and not faint – Hebrew "halak" means to fade away; to drive back; get rid of; go speedily.

This is a promise from God for those of us who look to the LORD with hope for the manifestation of the things we believe God for. There will come a day, if we do not faint, when what we believe for will happen.

Nehemiah knew he had a lot riding on his shoulder; so, he wisely waited for the LORD's timing.

The Appointed Time

Let us see how this period of waiting worked for Nehemiah.

Nehemiah 2:1-3 "[1]In the month of Nisan in the twentieth year of King Artaxerxes, when wine was brought for him, I took the wine and gave it to the king. I had not been sad in his presence before, [2] so the king asked me, "Why does your face look so sad when you are not ill? This can be nothing but sadness of heart." I was very much afraid, [3] but I said to the king, "May the king live forever! Why should my face not look sad when the city where my ancestors are buried lies in ruins, and its gates have been destroyed by fire?"

Scholars believe there must have been a banquet as the queen was sitting next to king Artaxerxes. Nehemiah went before the king to present the wine in the usual manner; yet his pain and burden for the dilapidated state of his countrymen weighed heavily on his heart. Here we see another quality Nehemiah possessed.

Consistency

He must have been a consistently cheerful individual and because of their long relationship, the king could tell from his demeanor that something was wrong. As many would say, Nehemiah wore his heart on his sleeve.

Something happened on this particular day that changed his countenance. He may have been discouraged and his heart became sad. He simply could not mask his feeling any longer.

Then he became afraid. In fact, scholars believe it could have been detrimental to Nehemiah for him to appear sad before the king of Persia. He could have been demoted, fired from his position, or bear some other severe consequence. Protocol for the king of Persia seemed very stringent in those days. A similar set of strict rules can be found in the story recorded in the Book of Esther in the Old Testament, when the king of Persia passed an edict to annihilate all the Jewish people in all the provinces in the land. Although Esther, who was a Jew, was his queen, she could not appear before him unless she was summoned. Eventually, she chose to risk her life to save her people.

Esther 4:9-11 "[9] Hathak went back and reported to Esther what Mordecai had said. [10] Then she instructed him to say to Mordecai, [11] "All the king's officials and the people of the royal provinces know that for any man or woman who approaches the king in the inner court without being summoned the king has but one law: that they be put to death unless the king extends the gold scepter to them and spares their lives."

Nehemiah seemed to be in a similar situation, so he became afraid when the king inquired why he was sad. This moment is when God would manifest His glory upon Nehemiah with favour. Sometimes, it is better for someone to ask what is bothering you rather than you telling them. If they ask, it is because they are interested in knowing.

In the first chapter, I mentioned that when God asks us to do something great for Him, He knows fear will attack us first. So, He will speak encouraging and assuring words to anchor our faith in Him. We are likely to hear His quiet voice in our spirit say, "Be not afraid." Such was the case when He said these words to:

The Virgin Mary

Luke 1:28-30 " [28] The angel went to her and said, "Greetings, you who are highly favoured! The Lord is with you." [29] Mary was greatly troubled at his words and wondered what kind of greeting this might be. [30] But the angel said to her, "Do not be afraid, Mary; you have found favour with God.""

In this case, God shares the position in which He sees Mary, and this startled her. He wanted to prepare her for the task ahead with these words of validation. Yet, she became afraid.

Jesus

Knowing Jesus was about to embark on His Ministry, while He was being baptized in the river Jordan, God said,

"This is my Son, whom I love; with him, I am well pleased." -Matthew 3:17

In the Book of Joshua, when Joshua took over the role of leadership from Moses, God gave him specific instructions to get His people ready to enter the land He had promised Moses. He further assured Joshua that every place his feet touched would belong to him. Yet, I noticed God had to repeatedly encourage Joshua not to be afraid but to be of good courage because He was with him. Even though God will call us for specific tasks, as I said in an earlier chapter, He would never ask us to do what He has not equipped us to do. As well, like Joshua, Mary,

David, Daniel, Moses and all the other great leaders in the Bible, God was with them all the way. Nehemiah was no different. We also have this guarantee from God.

Joshua 1:1-9 "After the death of Moses, the servant of the Lord, the Lord said to Joshua son of Nun, Moses' aide: ^{2}"Moses my servant is dead. Now then, you and all these people, get ready to cross the Jordan River into the land I am about to give to them—to the Israelites. ^{3} I will give you every place where you set your foot, as I promised Moses. ^{4} Your territory will extend from the desert to Lebanon, and from the great river, the Euphrates—all the Hittite country—to the Mediterranean Sea in the west. ^{5} No one will be able to stand against you all the days of your life. As I was with Moses, so I will be with you; I will never leave you nor forsake you. ^{6} Be strong and courageous, because you will lead these people to inherit the land I swore to their ancestors to give them. ^{7} "Be strong and very courageous. Be careful to obey all the law my servant Moses gave you; do not turn from it to the right or to the left, that you may be successful wherever you go. ^{8} Keep this Book of the Law always on your lips; meditate on it day and night, so that you may be careful to do everything written in it. Then you will be prosperous and successful. ^{9} Have I not commanded *you? Be strong and courageous. Do not be afraid; do not be discouraged, for the Lord God will be with you wherever you go.""*

Has God spoken to you about accomplishing a specific task or project that may seem daunting? Today He is saying these same words to you "Be strong and courageous. Do not be afraid; do not be discouraged, for the Lord your God will be with you wherever you go."

As we continue to review this Chapter, let us highlight some of the qualities displayed by Nehemiah:

Respect and Composure

Nehemiah responded to the king's query about his sadness with great composure, respect and wisdom. While afraid, he quickly blessed the king when he said, "May the king live forever!" before sharing his concern with the king. As a result, the king asked the long-awaited question, "What is it you want?" Nehemiah 2:4

I am impressed with the high level of training these Hebrew men received, no doubt, from their parents based on the respect they demonstrated to authority. Daniel, who was captured and sent in exile to Babylon greeted the king of Babylon in the same way after God spared his life when he was thrown into the lion's den.

Daniel 6:19-22 [19] At the first light of dawn, the king got up and hurried to the lions' den. [20] When he came near the den, he called to Daniel in an anguished voice, "Daniel, servant of the living God, has your God, whom you serve continually, been able to rescue you from the lions?" [21] Daniel answered, "May the king live forever! [22] My God sent his angel, and he shut the mouths of the lions."

In the end, both Daniel and Nehemiah received great favour from the king of Babylon and Persia respectively.

Game Changers can manage their attitude and control their emotions to achieve the highest good. Esther was offered half of the kingdom, in Daniel's case, the king of Babylon exalted Daniel's God over his entire nation. In his book "The Spirit of Leadership," Dr. Myles Munroe said, "the essence of leadership is not in techniques; it's in our attitude." [1]

We need to remember - *Proverbs 16:7 (NKJV) "When a man's ways please the Lord, He makes even his enemies to be at peace with him."*

Let us look at what happened with Nehemiah. This is a moment of truth for Nehemiah when God will manifest His favour upon him.

Nehemiah 2:4-6 "[4] The king said to me, "What is it you want?" Then I prayed to the God of heaven, [5] and I answered the king, "If it pleases the king and if your servant has found favour in his sight, let him send me to the city in Judah where my ancestors are buried so that I can rebuild it. [6] Then the king, with the queen sitting beside him, asked me, "How long will your journey take, and when will you get back?" It pleased the king to send me; so I set a time."

Total Reliance upon God

Nehemiah is also known as a man of prayer, as we will see throughout our study. Consistent with his character, we expect he would have thought through the details of his journey to Jerusalem should he receive favor with the king. Yet, when the king asked what he wanted, he sent a quick prayer quietly to God. He was totally dependent upon God. He stood before an earthly king who had the authority to provide him with the practical help he needed; however, he wisely sought direction from God, the King above all kings.

Relying on God for everything has been one of the toughest disciplines I had to learn as a Christian after occupying leadership roles in the corporate world for many years. I had grown accustomed to making decisions based on specific knowledge, guidelines and common sense. So, it was difficult for me to remember to seek God first when making decisions.

Before knowing God and kingdom dynamics as I do today, had I been placed in Nehemiah's position, I would have gone right ahead and shared my plan. Not so with this man of God. When we leave God out of the equation, we may get a good result but not the best result. Why settle for good when we can have the best?

Proverbs 3:5-6 (NKJV) [5] Trust in the Lord with all your heart and lean not on your own understanding; [6] In all your ways acknowledge Him, and He shall direct your paths."

You will notice that at the end, after receiving favour from the king, Nehemiah acknowledged and honoured God with these words in Nehemiah 2:8 …" And because the gracious hand of my God was on me, the king granted my requests."

Nehemiah 2:7-9 [7] I also said to him, "If it pleases the king, may I have letters to the governors of Trans-Euphrates, so that they will provide me safe-conduct until I arrive in Judah?" [8] And may I have a letter to Asaph, keeper of the royal park, so he will give me timber to make beams for the gates of the citadel by the temple and for the city wall and for the residence I will occupy?" And because the gracious hand of my God was on me, the king granted my requests. [9] So I went to the governors of Trans-Euphrates and gave them the king's letters. The king had also sent army officers and cavalry with me."

A Visionary and Solutionist

Nehemiah shared the problem with the king and he was ready to let the king know what he needed for the solution. This way, he did not guess, pause, or say, "Let me think about it." He was ready with the answer. He was alert and a forward thinker. He saw the big picture. Had he not been prepared; he might have lost the opportunity of a lifetime. What so many people in the world call "luck", is preparation meeting opportunity.

This situation has caused me to wonder how many times God has passed us over for something we could have done because we were not prepared. We have not studied or trained like an athlete who desires to win the goal medal at the Olympics or one who wishes to be top of their game by breaking records and being the best.

I challenge you to know that because of Christ, you can go the extra mile. You might be surprised at what you discover about God and yourself.

A Strategic Thinker

Nehemiah was able to scope the overall project of rebuilding the wall and installing the gates to be able to detail his needs for the long journey to Jerusalem. He would have recalled that during the time of Ezra when Zerubbabel and his teammate Joshua started to rebuild the temple, the governors of the Trans-Euphrates turned up and questioned them on who gave them authority. They promptly reported the matter to the king. Thank God that upon researching the record, they found that a previous king, Cyrus, had authorized the rebuilding of the temple and it was never completed. So, having a letter from the king addressed to the governors, was of paramount importance.

Ezra 5:2-4 [2] Then Zerubbabel son of Shealtiel and Joshua son of Jozadak set to work to rebuild the house of God in Jerusalem. And the prophets of God were with them, supporting them. ³At that time Tattenai, governor of Trans-Euphrates, and Shethar-Bozenai and their associates went to them and asked, "Who authorized you to rebuild this temple and to finish it?" ⁴ They also asked, "What are the names of those who are constructing this building?" 5 But the eye of their God was watching over the elders of the Jews, and they were not stopped until a report could go to Darius and his written reply be received."

Nehemiah knew he would be traveling through a forest with the kind of timber suitable for building the gates and his residence. He also asked for letters to support him in obtaining these supplies. He received everything he wanted and more. The king sent his army officials and cavalry to ensure his safety and enable him to arrive with all the official support as a representative of the king. Notice Nehemiah did not shy away from asking for what he wanted. Once he overcame his fright after praying to God, he became bold.

Courage and Boldness

When you know God has called you to complete a project or a task, no matter how daunting it may seem and how long it may take, He will always ask us to be strong, courageous, and not to be afraid. It takes courage, boldness, and a level of risk-taking to achieve greatness for God. "No Guts, No Glory." Our confidence must always be in God. He is the force that is greater than anything we can do. He is the one that would allow us to say, like the three Hebrew boys, "we will not bow."

Daniel 3:16-18 [16] Shadrach, Meshach, and Abed-Nego answered and said to the king, "O Nebuchadnezzar, we have no need to answer you in this matter. [17] If that is the case, our God whom we serve is able to deliver us from the burning fiery furnace, and He will deliver us from your hand, O king. [18] But if not, let it be known to you, O king, that we do not serve your gods, nor will we worship the gold image which you have set up.""

So, Nehemiah left the comforts of the king's palace to take an eight-hundred-mile journey through treacherous paths to follow through with God's plan for rebuilding not only the wall but also His people.

We have seen great leadership qualities in Nehemiah so far, yet the job is just about to begin.

Chapter 4

THE PLAN AND EXECUTION

Scoping the Project

Nehemiah arrived safely in Jerusalem and after being in the city for three days, he decided to take a tour of the wall. Being the wise man he was, he inspected the condition of the wall to obtain the scope of the work that would be required for the full restoration. He was gathering facts firsthand since up to this point, he had only received a report from his brother and other fellow Jews about its condition.

The corporate world uses this strategy in managing, which is referred to as "managing by facts" This is powerful as it takes out guessing or making assumptions. He astutely conducted this exercise at night as he had not met with any local officials to share his mission. In addition, he would not have wanted to raise speculation about him being there before he got started with his project. Since there were no gates with guards, he was free to travel around the city at night.

We know Nehemiah had been distressed about this situation; however, it is important to note he dealt with those emotions before God. Therefore, he did not rally the people in the city first because he was emotionally charged. Even though he empathized with his people's plight, he again showed composure. An effective leader cannot be led by emotions when developing a plan of action, especially when faced with a difficult challenge. This is not the time to seek to win a popularity contest. The focus must be on the end game, not on feelings. Armed with facts, he could develop a proper action plan to confidently present to the people.

Nehemiah 2:11-16 [11] *I went to Jerusalem, and after staying there three days* [12] *I set out during the night with a few others. I had not told anyone what my God had put in my heart to do for Jerusalem. There were no mounts with me except the one I was riding on.* [13] *By night I went out through the Valley Gate toward the Jackal Well and the Dung Gate, examining the walls of Jerusalem, which had been broken down, and its gates, which had been destroyed by fire.* [14] *Then I moved on toward the Fountain Gate and the King's Pool, but there was not enough room for my mount to get through;* [15] *so I went up the valley by night, examining the wall. Finally, I turned back and re-entered*

> *through the Valley Gate. [16] The officials did not know where I had gone or what I was doing, because as yet I had said nothing to the Jews or the priests or nobles or officials or any others who would be doing the work."*

Rally the Team

> *Nehemiah 2:17-18 [17] Then I said to them, "You see the trouble we are in: Jerusalem lies in ruins, and its gates have been burned with fire. Come, let us rebuild the wall of Jerusalem, and we will no longer be in disgrace." [18] I also told them about the gracious hand of my God on me and what the king had said to me. They replied, "Let us start rebuilding." So they began this good work."*

Nehemiah demonstrated his statesman quality when he addressed the people. Although they already knew the facts, he told them Jerusalem lied in ruins and its gates had been burned with fire. He commanded them to come – come out of their current state of mind; shift their thinking, follow him and he would show them the way. "Let us rebuild the wall of Jerusalem, and we will no longer be in disgrace," he said. Nehemiah 2:17.

With the force of the Spirit of God upon him, he delivered a very compelling appeal to them that enabled him to gain their confidence and ultimate support. It is important to note he said, "let us." He wanted them to know he was part of the team and part of the solution. This is music to my ears. He was a servant leader.

He made them feel significant again and showed them they could regain their dignity. They can rebuild the wall and deliver themselves from shame. There is a critical lesson to be learned. "Give a man a fish and you feed him for a day; show him how to fish and you feed him for a lifetime." Many companies have deployed this strategy by getting people at all levels of an organization involved in coming up with ideas to go forward with a particular project or to bring about certain changes. This approach causes everyone to have a stake in the outcome and feel a sense of accomplishment when the project is successfully completed.

Nehemiah exalted God before the people by letting them know how God had moved on the king's heart and the favour he received from him. In those days, once the king passed a law, it could not be repealed. Yet, Nehemiah had letters from the king to the governors of the Trans Euphrates for the people to see the Power of their God. Hope was restored and they were confident in knowing the Mighty Hand of God was upon them. Therefore, they agreed to start rebuilding without hesitation. It is important to note, they did not say, "We need to seek God for ourselves, after all, we do not know you. We know some of your relatives; but you did not come back with us. What makes you think you can get us out of this mess?" They did not demonstrate any fear and they did not ask for another meeting to set up committees. This demonstrates the influence Nehemiah quickly gained over the people of Israel.

This situation reminds me of when Jesus called His disciples. All He said was, "Come follow me and I will make you fishers of men." These businessmen left their work and immediately followed Jesus.

Mark 1:16-20 [16] *As Jesus walked beside the Sea of Galilee, he saw Simon and his brother Andrew casting a net into the lake, for they were fishermen.* [17] *"Come, follow me," Jesus said, "and I will send you out to fish for people."* [18] *At once, they left their nets and followed him.* [19] *When he had gone a little farther, he saw James son of Zebedee and his brother John in a boat, preparing their nets.* [20] *Without delay he called them, and they left their father Zebedee in the boat with the hired men and followed him."*

Nehemiah experienced this same compelling call from God to go up to Jerusalem to restore the wall.

There are times when God will call us to act either directly or indirectly. I pray that, like His disciples, Nehemiah and the people of Israel who met with Nehemiah, we will hear the special sound of the command and immediately obey.

I believe God is urgently calling disciples again, whom I refer to as Game Changers, to make a difference in our world.

The Clean Up Woman

I shared previously that I worked for one of Canada's largest financial institutions. In my earliest leadership roles, I was assigned to what I referred to as "clean up jobs." I would go into a branch where the operation was in chaos. Using the same strategy as Nehemiah, I quickly cleaned up the situation, only to be assigned to another one. After a while, my friends and I made fun of these assignments and I was labeled "the cleanup woman." I look back now and with a deep sense of humility, I recognize these assignments were training me for the future. Moreover, I acknowledge the gracious hand of God was upon me.

Opposition Revealed

Whatever matters to God sends the enemy into a frenzy. This situation is no different. As soon as the people came on board with Nehemiah and started the work, the enemy appeared on the scene.

Nehemiah 2:19-20 [19] But when Sanballat the Horonite, Tobiah the Ammonite official, and Geshem the Arab heard about it, they mocked and ridiculed us. "What is this you are doing?" they asked. "Are you rebelling against the king?" [20] I answered them by saying, "The God of heaven will give us success. We his servants will start rebuilding, but as for you, you have no share in Jerusalem or any claim or historic right to it.""

The enemy's tactic is to mock, intimidate, and ridicule the work at hand with the objective of weakening you so you can doubt God and abort the project and your destiny.

Sanballat the Horonite, Tobiah the Ammonite official, and Geshem the Arab would have also known that the king had stopped any building in Jerusalem; so, their first attack was to ask, "Are you rebelling against the king?" Little did they know God was already ahead of them and had given Nehemiah favour with the king.

When undertaking an assignment from God, it is essential to be resilient and resolute. Do not give in, do not give up, and do not give over. Again, Nehemiah exalted God before the people as he demonstrated his confidence in Him and that he would not be shaken by what men said. Furthermore, he let these three men know they are outsiders, and they would not have any part in this project, nor will they benefit from it.

Nehemiah 2:20 I answered them by saying, "The God of heaven will give us success. We his servants will start rebuilding, but as for you, you have no share in Jerusalem or any claim or historic right to it."

Nehemiah did not cower in fear or back down from their criticism. He dealt with them head-on. There are times when leaders need to ignore their critics and there are other times when they must confront them. Throughout, we have seen Nehemiah's close relationship with God and his constant reliance on God to know the appropriate course of action.

This chapter captures the astounding feat accomplished by Nehemiah. Considering the people in Jerusalem might have been living with the status quo for such a long time, they probably had lost all hope and motivation. The enemy bombarded them on every side. The thought of reconstructing the wall without help coming from outside their community could have been daunting.

However, Nehemiah skillfully:

1. Presented the facts and quickly casted a vision – the wall is in a dilapidated state, once we rebuild it, you will be out of disgrace.

2. Exalted God and shared about His goodness towards him.

3. Shared about the favour he received from the king.

He exercised compelling communication skills, astuteness and wisdom in his implementation strategy and timing of his presentation to the people, resilience and resolve in combating the opposition, plus continued trust in God.

Chapter 5

A Highly Organized Kick-Off

Nehemiah mobilized the people to start work on the wall with Eliashib the High Priest and his fellow priest leading the way at the Sheep Gate. This action by the High Priest showed strong support for Nehemiah as the people would be inclined to follow him and the priesthood. These leaders, led from the front.

Nehemiah 3:1-8 "Eliashib the high priest and his fellow priests went to work and rebuilt the Sheep Gate. They dedicated it and set its doors in place, building as far as the Tower of the Hundred, which they dedicated, and as far as the Tower of Hananel.[2] The men of Jericho built the adjoining section, and Zakkur son of Imri built next to them.[3] The Fish Gate was rebuilt by the sons of Hassenaah. They laid its beams and put its doors and bolts and bars in place.[4] Meremoth son of Uriah, the son of Hakkoz, repaired the next section. Next to him Meshullam son of Berekiah, the son of Meshezabel, made repairs, and next to him Zadok

> son of Baana also made repairs. [5] The next section was repaired by the men of Tekoa, but their nobles would not put their shoulders to the work under their supervisors.
>
> [6] The Jeshanah Gate was repaired by Joiada, son of Paseah and Meshullam son of Besodeiah. They laid its beams and put its doors with their bolts and bars in place. [7] Next to them, repairs were made by men from Gibeon and Mizpah—Melatiah of Gibeon and Jadon of Meronoth—places under the authority of the governor of Trans-Euphrates. [8] Uzziel son of Harhaiah, one of the goldsmiths, repaired the next section; and Hananiah, one of the perfume-makers, made repairs next to that. They restored Jerusalem as far as the Broad Wall.

Nehemiah inspired the people to agree to join him to rebuild the wall and demonstrated exceptional operations and people skills. There is no mention of how many people were involved. However, given the magnitude of the project with ten gates to be rebuilt and installed, one can imagine a large number of people were involved.

He quickly assessed his human resources, knowing them by name and title, whether they lived around the wall or outside the wall, their specific skills and assigned each group to reinforce the wall in the area they lived.

This was a very strategic move on Nehemiah's part as it meant each group would have a vested interest in repairing their area with a sense of pride. It would also keep them motivated to finish the job. Notice the priests were assigned to the Sheep Gate, which is the gate through which the sheep for sacrifice passed. As priests, they would be keen on having this gate installed as quickly as possible. Everyone was engaged, including the old and young, men and women, those with related skills, and those without. Whole families worked together - Nehemiah 3:12 "Shallum son of Hallohesh, ruler of a half-district of Jerusalem, repaired the next section with the help of his daughters."

Everyone got involved except the nobles for the Tekoites – Nehemiah 3:5 –"The next section was repaired by the men of Tekoa, but their nobles would not put their shoulders to the work under their supervisors."

A Committed Team

From all accounts, the people were stirred up and began with a determination to get the job done. Their hearts were intent on the job at hand. Nehemiah highlighted the zeal their fellowmen, Baruch, demonstrated as an example of the people's commitment towards this project.

Nehemiah 3:20 Next to him, Baruch son of Zabbai zealously repaired another section, from the angle to the entrance of the house of Eliashib, the high priest.

Every leader should be blessed with at least one Baruch on their team. Hopefully, this type of attitude would become contagious and spur on the team.

Everyone except the nobles mentioned in the paragraph above cooperated with Nehemiah's plan. Having such strong support no doubt made the job easier for him. Nehemiah was able to foster a spirit of teamwork amongst the people. This accomplishment further underscores the level of his people skills – the ability to work effectively with and through others.

Before continuing with Nehemiah's building project, I feel a strong sense to take you on a journey to examine the spiritual implications of the wall and gates as they relate to us individually and as leaders.

In the days of Nehemiah, cities were fortified by walls that were used to protect the inhabitants. These walls were usually very high and wide so that a sentinel could march along the top of the wall and watch over the city. In this position, he could identify misdemeanors inside and he could see on the outside if the enemy was approaching so he could set off the alarm.

There are times when walls must be built and there are other times when walls must be broken down. In the case with Nehemiah, the wall needed to be rebuilt and, in some places, restored to protect God's people and take them out of disrepair. However, under Joshua's leadership, when the Israelites had the daunting task of taking over the city of Jericho, they were faced with a wall that was tightly shut up. In this case, the wall had to be broken down for them to gain entry to the city. God gave them a most unique and unthinkable strategy for them to do so. Joshua 6:1-21

As leaders, it would be vital to ensure we are surrounded by the most important wall and that is Christ Himself as we remember we are the temple of God. The Sentinel on the wall is the Holy Spirit who would set off a spiritual alarm when sin is crouching at the gate of our soul.

God had this to say about Jerusalem at the time, which refers to us as a Church and individually today:

Zachariah 2:5 "And I myself will be a wall of fire around it,' declares the Lord, 'and I will be its glory within.'"

So often we include this passage of scripture in our prayers as though it is a given. However, God's promises are always conditional. Therefore, for Christ to wrap Himself around us as a wall of protection, our relationship with Him must be strong. We must always seek Him first. Nehemiah lived that lifestyle.

The Word of God says in 1 Corinthians 12 *"[12] So, if you think you are standing firm, be careful that you don't fall!"* As leaders, we must be very careful that as we grow in leadership and are promoted to higher levels of responsibility, we keep ourselves within the "wall". Not becoming so confident in our own strength that we move away from the Truth by the decisions we make. A study of King David's life shows that the more he was promoted, the more he worshiped God. The Bible records in 2 Samuel 6:14 that when the Ark of the Covenant was being transported to the City of David, he worshipped God with all his might even though he was king.

2 Samuel 6:14 "Wearing a linen ephod, David was dancing before the Lord with all his might."

Then there are walls to be broken down – unforgiveness, hurt and disappointments. These walls are set up as strongholds by the enemy and must be broken down if you are to be free to be the best leader for God. I urge you to bring them before God and ask Him to break down these walls in your soul and set you free. You may recall that Nehemiah did his own cleansing before God by asking forgiveness for not only his people but for himself and his family.

Gates play a vital part in the security of the wall. Everything came in and out of Jerusalem's gates - merchandise, animals and people, to name a few. The watchman at the gate decided who came in and who went out. When trouble loomed, the gates were shut and no one was allowed outside after dark. The gate is also a place where important decisions are made. In the book of Ruth, Boaz met with the elders at the city gate, established himself as kinsman-redeemer and settled the legal matter of his marriage to Ruth.

> *Ruth 4:11 "Then the elders and all the people at the gate said, "We are witnesses. May the Lord make the woman who is coming into your home like Rachel and Leah, who together built up the family of Israel. May you have standing in Ephrathah and be famous in Bethlehem."*

From a spiritual standpoint, we must be guarded about what we allow into our spiritual gates. Whatever is allowed in feeds our soul and will ultimately determine how we think, speak and function as leaders. What you meditate on, you will become.

After Moses' death God called Joshua to lead His people into the Promise Land. He knew the gigantic task Joshua would be undertaking; so, He encouraged him to be courageous. God gave him specific instructions that he had to follow to ensure his success.

Joshua 1:7-8 "[7] Be strong and very courageous. Be careful to obey all the law my servant Moses gave you; do not turn from it to the right or to the left, that you may be successful wherever you go. [8] Keep this Book of the Law always on your lips; meditate on it day and night, so that you may be careful to do everything written in it. Then you will be prosperous and successful.""

Let us consider the three key gates that feed our souls:

The **"eye gate"** - We now live in the information age when we can find information at our finger tips through various mediums. What we choose to look at on television, at the movies or on social media, could significantly impact how we think, reason, or behave. We must always ask the question, "Is what I am looking at glorifying God?"

The **"ear gate"** - This begs the question, "What do you listen to most of the time?

The **"mouth gate"** - Considering the mouth speaks according to what is in the heart, feeding the spiritual man with that which is wholesome would be an excellent place to start.

A focused leader would be selective in all the three areas while keeping their eyes on the vision. So did Nehemiah. We can imagine that once the rebuilding of the wall started, he continued to review his plan tweaking it where necessary, interacted with the people to hear what they had to say and encouraged them to keep at it.

Chapter 6

A Spiritual Journey Through the Gates

Let us take a look at the spiritual connotations of the ten gates that were repaired according to Nehemiah Chapter Three.

The Sheep Gate: Nehemiah 3:1

The Sheep Gate was given this name because the sheep for sacrifice were brought through this gate.1 At this gate, we remember that Jesus became the sacrificial lamb for us. It is the place where a decision would be made to change the course of one's direction.

We often become excited when someone introduces a great invention, breaks an existing record, or completes a significant project. However, we seldom give thought to the sacrifice the individual has made, the sleepless nights; the isolation from friends and sometimes family; the long, arduous work hours. It will cost you to become a Game Changer or a more impactful one.

Nehemiah was in a very comfortable place living at the palace. Yet, he gave it all up to roll up his sleeves, face ridicule and mockery to get his assignment done and make a difference for God and His people.

The Fish Gate: - Nehemiah 3:3

The Fish Gate was so-called because the fish from the Jordan and the sea of Galilee were brought through this gate into Jerusalem.[2] When 'fish' is mentioned in the scriptures, it usually refers to:

Provision– "the feeding of the five thousand" – Matthew 13:14-21 - and Jesus instructing Peter to collect a coin from the mouth of a fish to pay their taxes due – Matthew 17:27 - are two examples. May we also be reminded of the fact that God is the one who will provide whatever is needed for us to complete the assignment He has given us.

The mandate Jesus left us is for us to feed a hungry world with His Word. He told His disciples He would make them fishers of men – Matthew 4:19. As leaders, we are placed in positions of influence. The Fish Gate reminds us that we are to be witnesses of God wherever we are.

Matthew 10:32-33 [32]Whoever acknowledges me before others, I will also acknowledge before my Father in heaven. [33] But whoever disowns me before others, I will disown before my Father in heaven."

The Jeshanah (Old) Gate: – Nehemiah 3:6

Old speaks of that which is past. It also speaks of that which is solid and unchangeable like a foundation. There are many things labeled old that need renewing as well as many things that are old that should be discarded and quickly!3 As a leader, you must look to God for His guidance on when to build upon that which is old and when to bring something new to the table. As a Game Changer, you are not expected to maintain the status quo. Jesus could not teach His messages to the Sadducees and Pharisees. He said you could not put new wine in an old wineskin.

Matthew 9:17 "Neither do people pour new wine into old wineskins. If they do, the skins will burst; the wine will run out and the wineskins will be ruined. No, they pour new wine into new wineskins, and both are preserved."

We must be unafraid to remove old practices and habits or even rules contrary to God's Word to achieve the desired goal effectively. Sometimes, to bring about change in an organization, it is necessary to bring in new staff. In his autobiography, Lee Iacocca had this to say about the Vice Presidents in the Financial Department at Chrysler when he took over the presidency "the Vice Presidents were all square pegs in round holes."[4] This means they were not the best fit for their positions; therefore, they could not thrive and become strong contributors to the Company's success. In the end, he had to replace most of them. Nehemiah, on the other hand, was able to use the people he met in Jerusalem. They were enthusiastic about the project and were skilled and able to get the job done.

The Valley Gate: – Nehemiah 3:13:

This Valley Gate would be at a low point in the terrain around the city. It speaks of where we humble ourselves under the mighty hand of God and learn in the experience that Christ is my life. It is also the place of growing because growth generally does not come from the mountains. There are high places in our walk and testimony.

Remember, it takes two mountains to form a valley.[5] While the world seems to celebrate those who are boastful and proud under the auspices of being confident, the Word of God makes it abundantly clear that He resists the proud; but the humble He will exalt.

1 Peter 5:5 "In the same way, you who are younger, submit yourselves to your elders. All of you, clothe yourselves with humility toward one another, because, "God opposes the proud but shows favour to the humble."

One of the best ways for a leader to remain humble is to serve others.

The Dung Gate: – Nehemiah 3:14

This gate represents the place where all the city's refuse is brought to be discarded and burnt. Many times, God meets us in our valley experiences and as we yield to Him, He can take away the dross, the dung and the debris from our lives. Through these fiery furnace experiences, we can come out like pure gold. We can see the connection between the Valley Gate and the Dung Gate experiences. Galatians 5:19 lists some of the dung we must rid from our lives and replace with the Fruit of the Spirit.

Galatians 5:19-21 …"sexual immorality, impurity, and debauchery; [20] idolatry and witchcraft; hatred, discord, jealousy, fits of rage, selfish ambition, dissensions, factions [21] and envy; drunkenness, orgies, and the like."

We know of some leaders, inside and outside the Church, who either were unable to or simply did not eliminate some of these refuse in their lives. In the end, they were disgraced. As mentioned earlier, this is a lesson for all of us. It is not about pointing fingers. We all need to take heed, lest we fall.

Right now, I would like to ask the Holy Spirit to cleanse us once again from any dung that may remain in our lives and enable us to lead by a true example of who He is. May He enable us to develop the Fruit of the Spirit in us according to:

Galatians 5:22-23 "^{22} *But the fruit of the Spirit is love, joy, peace, forbearance, kindness, goodness, faithfulness,* ^{23} *gentleness and self-control."*

The Fountain Gate: – Nehemiah 3:15

The Fountain Gate reminds us of a fountain that springs up. It is so much like God to provide water to cleanse immediately after the valley and dung experiences. This fountain is Jesus. Through Him, we have hope; we are renewed and are kept refreshed. As leaders, we need to allow this Fountain to keep flowing in our lives. Through this experience, we will be filled with His joy that will be our strength to go the distance. Jesus said it this way:

John 7:38 "Whoever believes in me, as Scripture has said, rivers of living water will flow from within them."

We must also guard our heart or soul, for it is the wellspring of life.

Proverbs 4:23 "Above all else, guard your heart, for everything you do flows from it."

The Water Gate: – Nehemiah 3:26

The Water Gate was located near the Fountain Gate. Water in scripture refers to the Word of God. It is the Word of God that will illuminate our path; it is like a hammer and will crush to pieces the plans of the enemy against us. It is a two-edged sword that we can wield to the right and the left against the attacks that will come. Through the Word, the Blood and our Testimony, we overcome the enemy. Knowing the Word of God fills us with Wisdom. Knowing the Word of God and having the Wisdom of God will give you the edge as a Game Changer.

The Horse Gate: – Nehemiah 3:28

The Horse Gate represents warfare. The war horses would leave the city through the Horse Gate to be inspected for battle. Having gone through the Dung-gate,

Fountain gate and Watergate, we should be in a ready position for battle.[6]

The horse also speaks of discipline, strength, endurance and speed. These are all qualities of a Game Changer. To lead is to battle. There is the natural battle and the spiritual battle, whether you want them or not. In Chapter two of the Book of Nehemiah, we saw that it was not long before the opposer showed up. As we continue our study, we will see that he tends to show up at an opportune time just as he promised Jesus as he left him after the temptation in the wilderness – Luke 4:13. We must be sharp to his devices.

The East Gate: – Nehemiah 3:29

The East Gate was located east of the temple and is linked in Scripture with the rising sun. This is a picture of hope and expectation of the soon coming King. He is returning for a Church without spots and wrinkles and there is no question we have a lot of work to do. We must become passionate about rising up as true ambassadors of Christ. The world is groaning for sons of God to arise. God wants to do a new thing in our day. Let us not just read the Bible. Let us be representatives of the word of God recorded in the Bible and turn the world upside down for our LORD.

The Gate Miphkad (Inspection): – Nehemiah 3:31

The name miphkad is defined as an assignment, appointment, or numbering. We know one day we will have a performance appraisal from God that will take place at an appointed time. When we understand and accept that He created us for a purpose, we need to know the purpose or assignment to execute it according to His plan.

Even though Nehemiah was on the job in the king's palace, he somehow knew it was not his assignment from God. That was merely one of his training grounds.

It is my prayer that if you do not already know your assignment, you will ask the Holy Spirit to reveal it to you and He will. Once He does, like Nehemiah, you must obey.

This is the most challenging chapter I have written so far as I deliberated on the value and purpose of going through these gates. However, I hope that having gone through them, you will agree that God's blueprint for godly living is designed in an orderly fashion, just as He designed the earth.

Chapter 7

OVERCOMING OBSTACLES

As the building project continued, the enemy reappeared and manifested his opposition to the project in several ways. We read in Nehemiah chapter three that the people were fully engaged and rebuilding the wall at full speed with enthusiasm and commitment.

So often, we start a project, a new job, a new relationship, a new school, or a competitive sport with excitement and enthusiasm, filled with high hope for a successful journey to the finish line.

In this chapter, we will learn that life's path is seldom linear. It has curves, valleys, mountains and mishaps, to name a few. We can refer to this as the life cycle of anything we undertake. The good news is that God's Word stands forever and He has already declared that all things work together for good for those who love the LORD and are called according to His purpose. Furthermore, whatever the enemy means for evil, God will turn it around for good so that He may be glorified.

Since we have established that Nehemiah was an astute leader, he no doubt had a strategy in place to combat the enemies should they attack again. The good thing about Sanballat and Tobiah showing up so soon after the building project started is that Nehemiah got to know his enemies at a very early stage.

It is always good to know your enemy, opposition, rival, or competitor. Most democratically run countries have an Opposition Party and the existing government knows who that is. Companies spend a significant amount of money to study their competition and develop strategies, products and services to outdo them. The competition can spur you on to be your best or you can roll up the carpet and retreat.

A Game Changer would not retreat in time of battle or difficulty. Neither did Nehemiah. His faith in God and his resolve to complete the project kept him going. Here is what God has to say about those who retreat or shrink back:

Hebrews 10:38-39 "[38] but my righteous one will live by faith. My soul takes no pleasure in anyone who shrinks back." [39] But we are not among those who shrink back and so are lost, but among those who have faith and so are saved."

Friend or Foe

Viewed correctly, opposition or competition can be used as a catalyst to spur an individual or organization to be their best.

I recently read a fascinating document entitled "A Courtship of Rivals." about Larry Bird of the Boston Celtics and Irving "Magic" Johnson of the Los Angeles Lakers basketball teams. These two men were fierce rivals who used their rivalry to push them to become the best in their game.

It was reported that Larry Bird set out from the start of his career to position himself as Magic Johnson's opposition and he refused to speak to Magic Johnson (Magic). He branded Magic and went about with a single focus and determination to beat Magic at the game of basketball. Larry would carefully review and study every game Magic played so that he would learn how to improve his game and identify areas where he needed to do so.

Once Magic realized how serious Larry Bird was, he stepped up his game. Their rivalry on the basketball court attracted many viewers and electrified the game during their tenure.

One day, through a very unfortunate circumstance, Magic's career came to a sudden end. Around that time, Larry Bird was suffering from back injuries and had slowed down his game. Once Magic stopped playing, Larry lost his zeal to play. He no longer checked the plays. Before long, he too, ended his career. Today, they are great friends as they learned that in their rivalry, deep down in their hearts, they respected each other's prowess on the court and needed to challenge one another to get to the next level of their play.

A Real Enemy

From a spiritual perspective, we know we have a real enemy – Satan, whose plan is to steal, kill and destroy. He is also known as the Opposer. However, we are also told that if we anchor ourselves in Christ and resist Satan, he will flee – James 4:7. We also have a spiritual armor we can wear – Ephesians 6:10-18 - that will enable us to stand our ground.

Let us look at how the enemy attacked Nehemiah and the people.

Nehemiah 4:1-3 "When Sanballat heard that we were rebuilding the wall, he became angry and was greatly incensed. He ridiculed the Jews, [2] and in the presence of his associates and the army of Samaria, he said, "What are those feeble Jews doing? Will they restore their wall? Will they offer sacrifices? Will they finish in a day? Can they bring the stones back to life from those heaps of rubble— burned as they are?" [3] *Tobiah the Ammonite, who was at his side, said, "What they are building—even a fox climbing up on it would break down their wall of stones!""*

Sanballat's and Tobiah's attack was fueled by anger. In fact, Sanballat was incensed. So, we can imagine how vicious he would seek to be against God's people. He attacked their minds with words of ridicule and sent fiery darts of doubt to their hearts to explode and leave poison of fear and discouragement as he questioned their ability to get the job completed. This tactic was to break them down and cause them to give up. It is a mind game or psychological warfare used so often by the opposition in various aspects of life.

Nehemiah's Response

Nehemiah 4:4-5 [4] *Hear us, our God, for we are despised. Turn their insults back on their own heads. Give them over as plunder in a land of captivity.* [5] *Do not cover up their guilt or blot out their sins from your sight, for they have thrown insults in the face of the builders."*

Nehemiah followed a path he had used before. His first defense was a cry out to God. While there is no indication of the tone of his plea before God, I sense some anguish as he used the words, despised and insults to express to God how they were treated by their enemy. He went on to tell God how he would like to see them dealt with. "Turn their insults back on them"; "Give them over as a plunder in their land of captivity" – let them become captive to someone else. Do not forgive them.

You may question, how this great leader could ask God not to forgive his enemies when we are taught to love our enemies and do good to those who willfully despise us. In several of David's Psalms, he asked God to deal harshly with his enemies. We know whenever we cry out to God, He hears and answers.

Jeremiah 33:3 "'Call to me, and I will answer you and tell you great and unsearchable things you do not know.'"

Psalm 57:2 "I cry out to God Most High, to God, who vindicates me."

Managing Destructive Criticism

Hearing destructive criticism is never an easy thing for any of us. One of the things a leader can be sure of is that they will receive unfavorable criticism at some point in time. We know this kind of criticism, unlike constructive criticism, has a plan to steal your joy or confidence, kill your spirit and destroy your destiny.

We need to understand that part of any leadership package is criticism, whether you are a parent or CEO.

Anyone who steps into the arena of leadership must be prepared to pay the price. Real leadership exacts a heavy toll on the whole person. The more effective the leadership, the higher the price. Unpleasant as this may sound, you have not really led until you become familiar with the stinging barbs of the critics.1 This statement could not be more real than it is today. With social media at our fingertips, instant messaging and reporting are heightened.

It is, therefore, imperative for Game Changers to have thick skin and guard their hearts to ensure while they may hear criticism, they do not listen to it. Instead, they must listen to the voice of the Holy Spirit. Nehemiah did just that.

Can you imagine what it might be like today with a project of this magnitude? The scene would show your critics with their supporting cast ridiculing you, your workers and your project.

> *Nehemiah 4:1-2 When Sanballat heard that we were rebuilding the wall, he became angry and was greatly incensed. He ridiculed the Jews, [2] and in the presence of his associates and the army of Samaria, he said, "What are those feeble Jews doing? Will they restore their wall? Will they offer sacrifices? Will they finish in a day? Can they bring the stones back to life from those heaps of rubble — burned as they are?"*

In today's environment, this behaviour would attract crowds and reporters. Before long, it would become news on television and radio. People would put messages on social media and the story would go viral.

The broken-down walls in Jerusalem may be symbolic of the condition of one's life or an organization going through a rough patch. People on the outside looking on may feel superior in themselves or about their organization, for compared to you, they are much better off. What they would not know is that your Sovereign God can turn things around for His purposes in His time.

Like Sanballat and Tobiah, when God starts His rebuilding project in your life or your organization, onlookers begin to attack as they question and undermine your ability to rebuild strong. This kind of attack is fraught with jealousy, fear and arrogance. To them, if your building project succeeds, they would no longer be king of the heap. These were the same tactics the Jebusites used against David and his people.

2 Samuel 5:6 "The king and his men marched to Jerusalem to attack the Jebusites, who lived there. The Jebusites said to David, "You will not get in here; even the blind and the lame can ward you off." They thought, "David cannot get in here."

We know the result for David and we will study the result for Nehemiah. We must be confident in the fact that the end result for every God-assigned project we undertake is that we win!

Nehemiah continued to rally the team with a focused mind and the people gave it all they had and quickly reached halfway with building the wall.

Nehemiah 4:6 "So we rebuilt the wall till all of it reached half its height, for the people worked with all their heart."

This achievement enraged Sanballat and his team, so they escalated their attack. This time they threaten to fight against the people and stir up trouble. Nehemiah got wind of their threat and acted swiftly. He did what he had consistently done; he prayed and worked to avert the situation.

Nehemiah 4:9 "But we prayed to our God and posted a guard day and night to meet this threat"

Trouble in the Camp

Nehemiah had no sooner dealt with Sanballat and his team when the people from Judah and the Jews who lived nearby approached him with bad news.

Nehemiah 4:10-12 [10] Meanwhile, the people in Judah said, "The strength of the laborers is giving out, and there is so much rubble that we cannot rebuild the wall." [11] Also, our enemies said, "Before they know it or see us, we will be right there among them and will kill them and put an end to the work." [12] Then the Jews who lived near them came and told us ten times over, "Wherever you turn, they will attack us.""

Those "fiery darts" sent off by Sanballat and Tobiah seemed to have penetrated the minds of the people building the wall. They lost their joy and their will to finish the task even though they were already halfway done. They started to lose momentum and they became afraid. They saw the enemy bigger than themselves. They may have looked back and seen how much work they had already done and questioned whether they had enough strength left to complete the overwhelming task ahead of them.

There was another time in the history of God's people when they saw the enemy as giants and themselves only as grasshoppers – Numbers 13:27-33. Their report affected the entire nation of Israel and they never made it to the Promise Land – Numbers 14:20-23.

How we see ourselves in relationship to God and our enemy will determine whether we win or lose a battle.

The half-way point of a project or a distant journey can be a testing time for many. By this time, you have used a lot of energy and resources and are apt to question if you have done the right thing. This situation is further exacerbated when you hear negative comments about what you are involved with.

When we get to this juncture, it would be worthwhile to consider the following points:

- Have a focused and resilient leader who does not take their eyes off the goal and our sure foundation – God Almighty.

- Have positive thinking people around us to encourage us to keep fighting. Daniel had his three friends - Shadrach, Meshach, and Abednego.

- Encourage ourselves. David did so when his men threatened to stone him when the Amalekites raided their camp and took their wives, children, and livestock.

As a Christian, it is essential to remind ourselves of the past victories God has given us. These are our faith extenders.

Throughout this study, one thing that rings loud and clear is Nehemiah's devotion to God. He placed God first in everything he did.

Having experienced the manifestation of the power of God in his life through this project, Nehemiah never hesitated to call on God. However, notice while he does so, he also does what is practical. God will not do for us that which we can do for ourselves. He has given us talent, skills and abilities that we must use. When we walk closely with God as Nehemiah did, we do not always have to wait for some mysterious thing to happen to know what to do when there is a crisis. If your basement is flooded, you do not have to wait for God to tell you what to do.

Winning the Hearts of the Team Members

When a team is discouraged, a good leader seeks ways to encourage them. Nehemiah looked over the situation, perhaps against the plans he had drawn up and must have concluded the work that is left to be done is very doable; however, he needed his people to rise with strength and focus.

Having prayed to God, he stationed the people close to their families and equipped them with appropriate weapons. This strategy must have boosted their spirits a bit, for they now had weapons to defend themselves and their families. Then Nehemiah reminded them that God who is with them is faithful and awesome. By positioning them close to their families, he rallied them to fight for their families, wives, sons and daughters. He gave them a reason to fight other than just getting the wall finished. He gave them a purpose. He gave them a cause. Nothing moves people to action quicker than when they have these two elements operating in their lives – a purpose and a cause.

This action on Nehemiah's part clearly shows his brilliance as well as his ability to make decisions quickly and decisively and delegate effectively. He connected with his people's hearts. He encouraged them to keep God at the forefront of their minds and fight for their families, sons, daughters, wives and homes. They had significance and purpose. This was a clincher.

Nehemiah 4:13-23 [13] *Therefore, I stationed some of the people behind the lowest points of the wall at the exposed places, posting them by families, with their swords, spears and bows.* [14] *After I looked things over, I stood up and said to the nobles, the officials and the rest of the people, "Don't be afraid of them. Remember the Lord, who is great and awesome, and fight for your families, your sons and your daughters, your wives, and your homes."* [15] *When our enemies heard that we were aware of their plot and that God had frustrated it, we all returned to the wall, each to our own work. [16] From that day on, half of my men did the work, while the other half were equipped with spears, shields, bows and armor. The officers posted themselves behind all the people of Judah [17] who were building the wall. Those who carried materials did their work with one hand and held a weapon in the other, [18] and each of the builders wore his sword at his side as he worked. But the man who sounded the trumpet stayed with me. [19] Then I said to the nobles, the officials, and the rest of the people, "The work is extensive and spread out, and we are widely separated from each other along the wall. [20] Wherever you hear the sound of the trumpet, join us there. Our God will fight for us!*

[21] So we continued the work with half the men holding spears, from the first light of dawn till the stars came out.

[22] At that time, I also said to the people, "Have every man and his helper stay inside Jerusalem at night, so they can serve us as guards by night and as workers by day."

[23] Neither I nor my brothers nor my men nor the guards with me took off our clothes; each had his weapon, even when he went for water.

God frustrated the enemy's plans and caused the people to rise with faith in their hearts and fierce determination to get the project completed. Nehemiah acknowledged the work was extensive and spread out, so people were not working close to each other. As a result, he put a plan in place for them to know that when they heard the horn blow, he needed them to fight. He gave them clear instructions to follow. They worked day and night with swords either on their sides or in one hand. Nehemiah was right there in the trenches with them. Having him there with them during this time of crisis must have been very encouraging.

Chapter 8

CONFLICT RESOLUTION, RESOLVE AND VICTORY

Leadership is not for the faint of heart, particularly those in top-level positions. No sooner than Nehemiah implemented his strategy for completing the wall, he was presented with some most disheartening complaint about a practice being carried out by the wealthy and powerful nobles and officials. They were taking advantage of those who were less fortunate. Greed and corruption were being played out. So, there was a massive outcry from the people. To eat, stay alive and pay the taxes sanctioned by the king, they had no choice but to:

- Mortgage their properties.
- Borrow money.
- Sell their children into slavery.
- Pay interest.

This situation caused them to feel powerless against the powerful.

Nehemiah became enraged by this news, not only because of the stringent measures the nobles and officers had placed on their brothers; but because their actions violated God's will for His people. In Exodus 22:25, God told the people of Israel they were not to charge interest on money loaned to those in need. In Leviticus 25:35-36, 39-41, He addresses how to treat a countryman who becomes poor and sells himself as a slave. He is not to be treated as a slave but as a hired hand until the year of Jubilee when he shall be set free.

Nehemiah 5:1-5 [1] Now the men and their wives raised a great outcry against their fellow Jews. [2] Some were saying, "We and our sons and daughters are numerous; in order for us to eat and stay alive, we must get grain." [3] Others were saying, "We are mortgaging our fields, our vineyards and our homes to get grain during the famine." [4] Still others were saying, "We have had to borrow money to pay the king's tax on our fields and vineyards. [5] Although we are of the same flesh and blood as our fellow Jews and though our children are as good as theirs, yet we have to subject our sons and daughters to slavery. Some of our daughters have already been enslaved, but we are powerless, because our fields and our vineyards belong to others." [6] When I heard their outcry and these charges, I was very angry. [7] *I pondered them in my mind and then accused the nobles and officials."*

Nehemiah may have also been anguished by what could be construed as hypocrisy before God. On the one hand, he asked for God's favour and protection against his enemies while he built the wall and internally, the people were sinning against God who has been faithful to them. This would be a cause for God to turn against them. He may have recalled that a similar situation happened with Joshua when Achan sinned and caused them to lose a battle in Ai. (Joshua 7:1-16).

There are times leaders face situations that may cause them to become angry. We saw it happen to Jesus with the money changers in the temple. How they respond to these situations is very critical. We can be angry but do not sin – Ephesians 4:26. It is always best to take time out and quiet your soul. It is those times when you send a quick urgent call to God for his guidance and direction so you can deal with the matter in a composed and decisive manner.

After mulling the matter over in his mind, this no-nonsense leader called a meeting where he had everyone's attention. Since these practices were commonplace amongst Israel's people, Nehemiah needed to deal with the matter in public. He shared his findings and told them out rightly that what they were doing was wrong. He did not ask for their rationale for conducting these affairs in the manner they had done. They were wrong and he wanted them stopped.

Often in today's society, leaders become concerned about what is politically correct and compromise their values because they need to appease certain powerful individuals or groups. Consequently, ungodly practices are allowed, and we see the continuous moral decay in our society. In other instances, some leaders try to get the buy-in of everyone on the team before making a decision. At times, this process can prolong matters unnecessarily before a decision is made.

I agree there are times when this approach is beneficial. As leaders, we must be careful not to lead by consensus in areas where a firm and decisive decision needs to be made to benefit the overall team or the organization. Here is where we need the guidance of the Holy Spirit to know the difference.

Nehemiah used the direct approach, and I can imagine the firmness in his voice. The guilty parties quickly said they would stop their unfair and ungodly practices and do what Nehemiah asked of them.

Nehemiah did not leave it up to them to follow through. He called the priests before the people and had the nobles and officials take an oath to carry out their promise. He put in place some accountability measures. To demonstrate the seriousness of this oath, he shook out the folds of his robe as an indication of how God would shake out their houses and possessions if they did not keep their promise. This must have put the fear of God in their hearts.

> *Nehemiah 5:12-13* [12] *So they said, "We will restore it, and will require nothing from them; we will do as you say." Then I called the priests, and required an oath from them that they would do according to this promise.* [13] *Then I shook out the fold of my garment and said, "So may God shake out each man from his house, and from his property, who does not perform this promise. Even thus may he be shaken out and emptied." And all the assembly said, "Amen!" and praised the Lord. Then the people did according to this promise."*

Unfortunately, stories like this one have happened to mankind through the ages where those in power come against their own people and carry out similar or worst atrocities against them.

As leaders, we must be mindful to treat our fellow men with grace and dignity regardless of their station in life. I hold the words of God in Micah 6:8 as a guiding post in the way I handle difficult situations with individuals.

Micah 6:8 "He has shown you, O mortal, what is good. And what does the Lord require of you? To act justly and to love mercy and to walk humbly with your God."

Along with the other great leadership qualities Nehemiah has already demonstrated, we note his acuteness at judging situations and bringing about a quick resolution.

Nehemiah went on to share how he had conducted himself since he was made Governor of the Province. He lent money to some people; paid his way and did not use any benefits allotted to him. He provided meals for approximately 150 Jews and officials daily as well as those who visited from other nations. He stood before the people as an example of a man of integrity and generosity. Because of how he conducted himself, he asked for God to remember him with His favour.

Nehemiah 5:19 "Remember me with favour, my God, for all I have done for these people."

Nehemiah's actions in addressing the situation amongst the people were the beginning of restoring the people and putting order in place. Order precedes Glory.

Back to the Building Project

While Nehemiah settled the dispute amongst the people, the building of the wall continued. Just as he had a strategy to rebuild the wall, the opposition had a strategy to destroy the wall.

Nehemiah kept a keen eye on the progress of the building with full knowledge that he had real opposition. However, he had a strong ally in God.

Various Tactics of Distractions

Realizing that all their efforts so far to thwart the plans for rebuilding the wall were foiled, Sanballat and his team came up and started a soft and seemingly friendly approach towards Nehemiah. It was not long before their nature manifested. Here are some of the activities they deployed against Nehemiah and his response:

1. Sanballat extended an invitation to Nehemiah for a meeting. Nehemiah realized they intended to harm him, so his response to them was that he is involved with a great project

and could not leave to meet with them. Sanballat was persistent with his invitation, which he extended four times and each time Nehemiah's response was the same. He was too engaged with his project to spend time with the opposition. As leaders, we need the wisdom of God and discernment of the Holy Spirit to know how to respond to the opposition's invitation.

2. Sanballat sent a letter accusing Nehemiah that he and the Jews were rebuilding the wall because they were plotting a revolt and Nehemiah would become their king. This would be a direct affront to king Artaxerxes and was a way for them to continue their intimidation tactics.

Nehemiah could see through their plot so he quickly refuted their accusation. He realized they were trying to frighten them so they can become weak. He did what he always did, which is to cry out to God to strengthen their hands.

As a leader, when accused of something you know to be absolutely false, although emotionally it may hurt at first, like Nehemiah, you can defuse the lie by ignoring it. Press on with faith and courage to get the job done and remember to cry out to God for help.

Nehemiah visited Shemaiah, the prophet, at his home. Obviously, he trusted this man. Shemaiah advised him that people were plotting to kill him so he should let them go to the temple to hide. Being devoted to God, Nehemiah refused this suggestion for having come this far, to hide would indicate that, a) He no longer trusted God to preserve and protect him to see the project to the end and b) He would sin against God by going into the temple as only priests were allowed to go into the temple sanctuary. Numbers 3:10; 18:7

If Nehemiah caved into this threat and ran in hiding, the opposition would have been able to claim he had a weak spot because he was afraid to lose his life. In addition, they would be able to discredit him as a strong leader. Furthermore, going into the temple to hide would have caused him to sin against the God he served and bring into question his credibility. They would no doubt take this as an opportunity to slander his name amongst the people.

I cannot begin to imagine Nehemiah's emotional state after these many attacks, plus the betrayal of a trusted man. He later found out there were traitors amongst his people from Judah. They passed information to the enemy's camp via Tobiah, who repeatedly sent letters to intimidate Nehemiah. Consistently Nehemiah called out to his defender – God Almighty. His faith in God was unquestionable. He had true grit!

Victory at Last

Nehemiah continued his building project and did the unthinkable. He and his team finished the project in a record fifty-two days. Glory to God!

This achievement shocked not only his opponents but also people in the neighbouring nations. Fear gripped their hearts and they lost their self-confidence. They realized that all along, as they fought Nehemiah, they had been fighting against God.

Nehemiah 6:16 "When all our enemies heard about this, all the surrounding nations were afraid and lost their self-confidence, because they realized that this work had been done with the help of our God."

This has been an incredible fifty-two days. The attacks

started as soon as Nehemiah reached Jerusalem and there was no let-up. I am convinced that the differentiating factor for Game Changers who know God is that they will indeed do mighty exploits.

Since Moses had seen the amazing miracles of God, when God asked him to lead His people into the wilderness, Moses asked God to show him His Glory to make a distinction between His people and the others. So, God granted Moses his request. I believe God will show His Glory throughout the earth through His people. He is looking for people who would trust Him like Nehemiah, Daniel, David, Shadrach, Meshach and Abednego through whom He can display His Glory. How about you and me?

Exodus 33:12-18 [12] *Moses said to the Lord, "You have been telling me, 'Lead these people,' but you have not let me know whom you will send with me. You have said, 'I know you by name, and you have found favour with me.'* [13] *If you are pleased with me, teach me your ways, so I may know you and continue to find favour with you. Remember that this nation is your people."* [14] *The Lord replied, "My Presence will go with you, and I will give you rest."* [15] *Then Moses said to him, "If your Presence does not go with us, do not send us up from here.* ¹⁶ *How will anyone know that you are pleased with me and with your people unless you go with us? What else will distinguish me and your people from all the other people on the face of the earth?"* ¹⁷ *And the Lord said to Moses, "I will do the very thing you have asked, because I am pleased with you and I know you by name."* ¹⁸ *Then Moses said, "Now show me your glory."*

Chapter 9

THE WRAP UP

Re-establishing the People

One would think that once the wall was rebuilt, Nehemiah's job was finished, since that seemed to be his initial focus. However, once he got on the job, he realized there was another building project he also needed to complete. He had to put structure and order in place to properly re-establish God's people in Jerusalem by taking these actions:

1. His first order of business was to appoint the worship team and the priests. With Nehemiah it was always God first.

2. Then, he appointed his brother Hanani along with Hananiah to oversee Jerusalem. The qualifications these two men possessed caused them to be placed in this position were their integrity and fear of God. Nehemiah was reproducing

after his own kind. Perhaps he said about them, "these are men after my own heart".

3. After, he gave instructions regarding the security of the city as it relates to the opening and closing of the gates, he appointed guards. Having experienced many attacks while he built the wall, Nehemiah would be mindful that even though the enemies seemed to have become quiet, they were still very much alive. Therefore, having security in place quickly would be of paramount importance.

Nehemiah 7:1-3 After the wall had been rebuilt and I had set the doors in place, the gatekeepers, the musicians, and the Levites were appointed. [2] I put in charge of Jerusalem my brother Hanani, along with Hananiah, the commander of the citadel because he was a man of integrity and feared God more than most people do. [3] I said to them, "The gates of Jerusalem are not to be opened until the sun is hot. While the gatekeepers are still on duty, have them shut the doors and bar them. Also appoint residents of Jerusalem as guards, some at their posts and some near their own houses."

In his position as governor, God laid it on Nehemiah's heart to assemble the nobles, officials and all others for registration by families. He looked at their genealogy on record and accounted for approximately 50,000 people. They also counted their livestock. This exercise would have given Nehemiah an idea of the people living in Jerusalem, their tribes and the health of the priesthood. It would also show the strength of the city and the resources they had. Besides, it would have shown the people that order was being put into place.

Quite often, when a leader takes over a new job, the first thing they do is to assess their human resources to determine their talents, capabilities and positioning in the organization. Armed with this information, they can put a proper structure in place and ensure the right people are in the right positions.

A Watershed Moment at Watergate

Nehemiah 8:1-4 [1] all the people came together as one in the square before the Water Gate. They told Ezra the teacher of the Law to bring out the Book of the Law of Moses, which the Lord had commanded for Israel. [2] So on the first day of the seventh month Ezra the priest brought the Law before the assembly, which was made up of men and women and all who were able to understand. ³ He read it aloud from daybreak till noon as he faced the square before the Water Gate in the presence of the men, women and others who could understand. And all the people listened attentively to the Book of the Law. ⁴ Ezra the teacher of the Law stood on a high wooden platform built for the occasion.

Nehemiah gathered the people in a square outside the Water Gate and they asked asked Ezra to read to them from the Book of the law of Moses.

This desire in the people's hearts to hear the Word of God must have been initiated by God. He had restored their wall and gates, settled them in the city, re-established the priesthood and now He wanted to restore His people. This is a time when God would meet His people right where they were.

Ezra opened the Book of the Law of Moses and praised God by acknowledging Him as the great God. The people lifted their hands and responded "Amen! Amen! Then they bowed down and worshipped the LORD with their faces to the ground.

Nehemiah 8:5-6 ⁵ Ezra opened the book. All the people could see him because he was standing above them, and as he opened it, the people all stood up. ⁶ *Ezra praised the Lord, the great God; and all the people lifted their hands and responded, "Amen! Amen!" Then they bowed down and worshiped the Lord with their faces to the ground."*

They listened intently to what Ezra read and gained an understanding from the Levites, who were their interpreters. Many of them would have needed what was said in Hebrew to be translated because they were born while in exile and would not have been proficient in their mother tongue.

When they understood the Word and realized how far they had moved from the laws God had given them through Moses, they wept bitterly. Nothing can penetrate the heart of man more than the Word of God, either spoken, written or in song. It was a time of cleansing, a time when God restored His people unto Him. Yes, they were free from captivity; but they were still held captive in their hearts as they practiced many pagan ways. Hearing and learning the Truth set them free.

Nehemiah 8:8-11 ⁸ *They read from the Book of the Law of God, making it clear and giving the meaning so that the people understood what was being read.* ⁹ *Then Nehemiah the governor, Ezra the priest and teacher of the Law, and the Levites who were instructing the people said to them all, "This day is holy to the Lord your God. Do not mourn or weep." For all the people had been weeping as they listened to the words of the Law. [10] Nehemiah said, "Go and enjoy choice food and sweet drinks, and send some to those who have nothing prepared. This day is holy to our Lord. Do not grieve, for the joy of the Lord is your strength."*

[11] The Levites calmed all the people, saying, "Be still, for this is a holy day. Do not grieve."

Once they understood the Word of God, Nehemiah, Ezra and the Levites (priests) encouraged them to stop weeping, for it was a day that was Holy to the LORD their God. They should not grieve for the joy of the LORD would strengthen them. Having the joy of the LORD would have been an indication that God is forgiving; therefore, they can enjoy themselves in His presence.

A great feast was put before the people and they celebrated for seven days. The people of God had not celebrated in this fashion since the days of Joshua. God's people were renewed, refreshed and restored. Each day Ezra read from the book; the people gathered to listen.

Nehemiah 8:17 "The whole company that had returned from exile built temporary shelters and lived in them. From the days of Joshua son of Nun until that day, the Israelites had not celebrated it like this. And their joy was very great."

This Feast of the Tabernacle is still recognized amongst the Jewish people today.

The gathering of God's people, reading of His Word, repentance of His people and celebration underscores Nehemiah's ability to be a big thinker who not only looks at the immediate, but looks at the big picture. As I mentioned in the early part of this chapter, the assignment was not only about building the wall, but it was also about building God's people. Nehemiah was not self-centered. He understood the protocol. He stepped aside and called Ezra to read the Book to the people, which was appropriate for him to do in his role as priest. Doing so did not detract from Nehemiah's position as governor.

A good leader will call in experts for jobs where they do not have specific expertise and garner the best for the company. Nehemiah led by example. We have established he was devoted to God and he would have it no other way but to use his position of influence, as governor, to point the people to God.

A Time of Repentance

Nehemiah's work of building the people did not end with this celebration. Later in the same month, the people gathered for a time of cleansing and confession of their sins. God was using Nehemiah to clean camp because His people had inter-married and embraced many pagan practices. He could not let this remain. Today, we know God is coming back for a church without spot and wrinkle.

After a lengthy prayer and confession of their sins and sins of their forefathers, similar to how Nehemiah prayed in his first recorded prayer, the people agreed to the following:

- Walk in God's law.
- Observe and do all the commandments of the Lord.
- Keep His judgment and statutes.
- Not marry foreigners.
- Not to make purchases on the Sabbath and Holy day.
- Observe the seventh year as one of rest.

- Pay 1/3 shekel each to the temple annually.

- Supply wood for the temple.

- Give all the first fruit offering to the priest.

- Observe the law of the firstborn. (Exodus 13:2)

- Tithe on all income.

- Not to forsake the house of God.

This was a systematic process of rebuilding the people. The agreement was put in place and the people had consecrated themselves to the LORD to establish them in the city.

When the exiles returned from Persia, many settled in neighbouring towns outside Jerusalem because the wall was broken. So, there were many vacant spaces in the city as there were only a few inhabitants.

The leaders who lived in Jerusalem invited one in every ten people to return to the city now that the wall was rebuilt, the gates in place and security set up. Several responded to this invitation and moved to Jerusalem.

Nehemiah 11:1-2 "Now the leaders of the people settled in Jerusalem. The rest of the people cast lots to bring one out of every ten of them to live in Jerusalem, the holy city, while the remaining nine were to stay in their own towns. ² The people commended all who volunteered to live in Jerusalem."

Dedication of the Wall of Jerusalem

Nehemiah 12:27-30 ²⁷ At the dedication of the wall of Jerusalem, the Levites were sought out from where they lived and were brought to Jerusalem to celebrate joyfully the dedication with songs of thanksgiving and with the music of cymbals, harps and lyres. ²⁸ The musicians also were brought together from the region around Jerusalem—from the villages of the Netophathites, ²⁹ from Beth Gilgal, and from the area of Geba and Azmaveth, for the musicians had built villages for themselves around Jerusalem. ³⁰ When the priests and Levites had purified themselves ceremonially, they purified the people, the gates and the wall."

With everything in place, it was now time to dedicate the wall. Nehemiah organized an elaborate dedication ceremony. This is not surprising yet consistent with how we have seen him do things; he would desire to give his best to God. Moreover, his opposition would hear about it and know his God is unstoppable:

- He sought out and brought in the Levites from the towns where they lived.

- He brought in musicians from the surrounding provinces.

- He organized two choirs.

The Dedication Ceremony

The long-awaited day came for the dedication of the priests, the people, the wall and the gates. I cannot begin to imagine the eager anticipation of the people, the exuberant joy in their hearts and the smiles that beamed across their faces. It makes me think of that day when Jesus will come again to gather His saints to be with Him forever.

The plans were already laid out and theses activities took place:

- The priests, people, wall and gates were purified.

- Ezra led a procession around the wall,

followed by the choir, the leaders of Judah, some priests with trumpet and the musicians.

- Choirs marched on top of the wall in the opposite direction while singing songs of thanksgiving.

- Choirs met at the end of the procession and proceeded to the House of God where they took their place.

- Nehemiah, half the officials and the priest also took their places in the House of God.

- Offerings of sacrifices were given.

- Individuals were appointed to carry out specific duties in the House of God.

This was a glorious day for the people of Jerusalem. They were filled with great joy and the sound of their rejoicing could be heard far away. I can imagine them shouting, "Victory! Victory! Victory!" At last, this was a great honour to God and a demonstration of the manifestation of His Glory!

Nehemiah 12:43 "And on that day they offered great sacrifices, rejoicing because God had given them great joy. The women and children also rejoiced. The sound of rejoicing in Jerusalem could be heard far away."

Mission Accomplished

After several arduous years, Nehemiah's assignment was completed. He rebuilt the wall and God's people with the gracious help of God. There can be no question that Nehemiah was a Game Changer. Under his leadership, God's people no longer lived in despair and disgrace. The following are his key accomplishments as he:

1. Inspired and mobilized the people to rebuild the wall against constant and severe opposition.

2. Established a structure for securing the wall.

3. Resolved conflict amongst the Jewish people where the nobles and officials were oppressing the needy.

4. Reinstated the Priesthood and the musicians.

5. Pointed the people to God through the reading of His Word, the Book.

6. Reinstated the "Feast of the Tabernacle," which had not been celebrated since Joshua's time.

7. Consecrated the people to God.

8. Established an Agreement with the people to uphold the laws and statutes of God and not to forsake God.

9. Increased the population in the City of Jerusalem by invitation.

10. Dedicated the wall and the people.

This was a tremendous undertaking with an exceptional performance appraisal. The results should convince us that with God, all things are possible.

Nehemiah's Departure and Return

After being governor for twelve years and everything was put in place, Nehemiah returned to Persia. Sometime later, he returned only to discover that aspects of the Agreement the people had signed were broken. This greatly displeased him.

> *Nehemiah 13:6-9 "But while all this was going on, I was not in Jerusalem, for in the thirty-second year of Artaxerxes king of Babylon I had returned to the king. Sometime later I asked his permission [7] and came back to Jerusalem. Here I learned about the evil thing Eliashib had done in providing Tobiah a room in the courts of the house of God. [8] I was greatly displeased and threw all Tobiah's household goods out of the room. [9] I gave orders to purify the rooms, and then I put back into them the equipment of the house of God, with the grain offerings and the incense."*

However, in Nehemiah's style he wasted no time in bringing about the necessary reforms. Some of the things that happened were:

Eliashib, the priest, allowed Tobiah, one of the key opposers to the building of the wall, to have a room in the courts of God, which was utterly displeasing to Nehemiah. He referred to this action as evil on the priest's part.

The promises made to support the Levites and the singers were broken. This caused them to leave their positions in the temple and return to work in the fields.

Some of the Jews had married foreign wives and their children spoke an impure language. He was so enraged by the lifestyle of the people that he pronounced a curse on them and pulled out some of the men's hair.

The Sabbath was not upheld as people were trading on that day.

The situation Nehemiah met upon his return, mirrors what happened to the Jews during the time of the Judges. They would cry out for help; God sent a judge and they repented; then they started to do what they thought was right in their own eyes and moved away from God; then they called out to Him again and He sent help.

I thank God He is the same yesterday, today and forever. (Hebrews 13:8). For many have fallen by the wayside, but He made a way through His Son Jesus Christ that we may come to Him, ask for forgiveness and be restored.

Chapter 10

THE QUALITIES AND CHARACTERISTICS OF A GAME CHANGER

As I studied the Book of Nehemiah, I identified and underlined several qualities and characteristics he possessed that made him an outstanding Game Changer. In chapter two I surmised the types of qualities I believe Nehemiah had that would qualify this Jewish man to be a cupbearer for a powerful pagan king. Now we have seen him in action, we can clearly identify those qualities.

History has recorded many great Game Changers. I believe the differentiating factor for Christians is the glorious benefit of being connected to God through His Son Jesus Christ. Once we know Him, His glory will manifest through us and like Nehemiah, we will be unstoppable concerning the will of God for our lives and His kingdom purposes.

For easy references, I provide below a recap of the skills, qualities and characteristics demonstrated by Nehemiah that I have outlined throughout the book in the order they appear.

Visionary and Solutionist

Strategic Thinker

Courage and Boldness

Compelling Communications Skills

Astuteness and Wisdom

Resilience and Resolve

Trust in God

Exceptional Operations and People Skills

Foster a spirit of Teamwork

Make decisions quickly and decisively

Delegate effectively

Let us now look at some key differentiating factors that set Nehemiah apart as a great Game Changer leader.

God Fearing

This quality is the most outstanding and important one Nehemiah possessed. God was "top of mind" for him. He readily confessed sins, called on God for help, told God how to deal with his enemies and asked for God's favour.

He was fastidious about the things of God and was intolerant of those who violated them. This was evident when he dealt with the conflict between the nobles and officials as well as the people and individuals who intermarried foreigners when he returned to Persia.

He not only upheld himself to a high standard when it came to the laws laid down by Moses, but he also called on the people he led to follow suit. Nehemiah was a shining model of a godly man.

A Visionary and Solutionist

Nehemiah saw the end state of the project before he began. An architect sees a potential building in its complete state; then, he starts his drawings until his vision is manifested. Nehemiah was a cupbearer, but he never lost his love and concern for his fellowmen in Jerusalem. Because they are God's chosen people, his vision was one that saw them thriving and doing well. He saw them prospering – nothing broken, nothing needs to be fixed.

The news that this was not the case was heart-wrenching for him. Instead of what he saw in his mind's eye for them, they were in disrepair and disgrace. Like Daniel, the moment he learned the situation was different, he cried out to God and asked for the king's favour.

Visionaries think beyond themselves. Nehemiah's concern was about the condition of his fellowmen in Jerusalem and the representation of God.

Proverbs 29:18 (KJV) "Where there is no vision, the people perish: but he that keepeth the law, happy is he."

Courageous and Bold

He was unafraid to take on a project as massive as rebuilding Jerusalem's wall. He had never been to Jerusalem before, but his faith was rooted in God.

Proverbs 28:1 "The wicked flee though no one pursues, but the righteous are as bold as a lion."

Humble

He did not think that because he held a high position in the king's court and had a connection with the king, the favour would have been automatic. He sought help from God. Also, during the building of the wall, he rolled up his sleeves and was in the trenches with the workers.

Wise

Nehemiah exhibited the supreme wisdom of God when dealing with his opposers, who repeatedly tried to distract him from getting the job done.

A Risk-taker

He was prepared to leave his comfortable surroundings in the king's court to go to Jerusalem to undertake a massive project and work with people he did not know. Moreover, they were in disarray and despair, so there was a possibility they would not cooperate with him.

Resilient and Resolute

Nehemiah dealt with attacks from the opposition outside the wall, discouragement amongst the workers and conflict amongst the people. Midway into the building project, the people wanted to give up. Yet, he never backed down and with God, the wall was built in a record time of fifty-two days.

Outstanding People Skills

People are the greatest asset of any organization or project. While we do not know precisely how many people participated in building the wall, given the size of the project, we can imagine hundreds of people were involved. Nehemiah handled the many personalities and issues that arose, kept them focused and finished the job in record time with help from the Almighty God.

A Man of Integrity

As governor, Nehemiah was entitled to monetary and other benefits. Unlike his predecessors, he did not avail himself of these benefits. Instead, he funded his own cost of living and supported and hosted up to 150 people daily for a meal. He realized that to do otherwise, would place a burden on his people.

An Outstanding Project Manager

From the onset, Nehemiah received favour from the king to leave his position as cupbearer to pursue another assignment. The king repealed a law that prohibited any building from being completed in Jerusalem and provided him with letters for safe travel from Persia to Jerusalem and obtain supplies along the way. In addition, he provided security.

When he arrived in Jerusalem, Nehemiah mobilized the people to rebuild the wall; staved off and overcame his opposition; resolved conflicts amongst the people; turned the people back to God; re-established the work of God in the temple and kept God at the center of his project at all times.

There can be no question that God was with Nehemiah. In a practical way, regardless of the position you hold in life, having studied the life of Nehemiah, I trust you will learn how to:

- Pray when faced with difficult situations that are beyond your ability to resolve.

- Rely totally on God and, at the same time, do the practical. Pray and keep going.

- Resolve conflicts.

- Inspire people to become motivated to

continue with the job when morale is low.

- Handle destructive criticism and discouragement.

- Set goals and follow through with the action plan when difficulties arise to cause you to get off track.

- Remain humble when promoted and keep integrity intact.

- Stand firm when faced with difficult situations and trust God.

Our world today desperately needs Game Changers. Now that you have read about Nehemiah, as the example of a Game Changer and observed the many qualities he had; will you volunteer to develop and or nurture these necessary characteristics to stand as a Game Changer? I hope you are now poised to fulfill this goal. I encourage you to complete the following three actions:

1. Complete a self-evaluation for each of the qualities Nehemiah displayed.

2. Establish at least two goals for

yourself to bring about changes to ensure you become a godly Game Changer.

3. As you intentionally and purposefully develop into a great Game Changer leader, I encourage you to help others to do likewise.

Make a decision today!

Questions for you:

1. What are some Game Changer qualities that Nehemiah possessed which you would like to develop and how would you reach this goal?

_____
_____
_____
_____
_____
_____
_____
_____

2. What did you learn from how Nehemiah approached the king and gained his favour? How would you apply this to your life?

_____
_____
_____
_____
_____
_____
_____
_____
_____

3. Based on how Nehemiah rallied the people in Jerusalem to build the wall, how would you approach your team to get them to buy in to your project?

_____
_____
_____
_____
_____

4. How would you handle people who overtly oppose your project as Sanballat and Tobiah did to Nehemiah?

5. What pattern did Nehemiah followed throughout the project of rebuilding the wall you would apply to any project you would undertake?

Notes

Chapter 1

1. www.oxfordlearnersdictionaries.com
2. www.investopedia.com

Chapter 2

1. 1 Charles R Swindoll "Hand Me Another Brick" pg 6
2. 2 Charles R. Swindoll "Hand Me Another Brick", pg 11

Chapter 3

1. 1 Dr. Myles Munroe "the Spirit of Leadership", pg 44

Chapter 6

1. Dake's Annotated Reference Bible
2. Dake's Annotated Reference Bible
3. www.godfire.net/rayknight - re-think No.78
4. Autobiography by Lee Iacocca pg 155
5. www.godfire/rayknight -re-think No.78
6. Alfred E. Bouter 2004 (Printed/Updated March 31, 2005

Chapter 7

1. Charles R. Swindoll "Hand Me Another Brick", pg65

About the Author

Dr. Innes' career with Canada's leading financial institution spanned four decades. During that time, she held several leadership positions involving Branch Management, Operations, Human Resources and Finance.

She later joined the Pastoral team at Kingdom Covenant Ministries and was responsible for Care and Home Groups. Dr. Innes held the position of Vice Chancellor and Professor at Kingdom Covenant Leadership Institute overseeing the operations for the local and affiliate campuses in the USA and the Caribbean as well as Online. She gained her doctoral degree in Christian Leadership and Management from Kingdom Covenant Leadership Institute and her Master's degree in Theology from Christian Life School of Theology in the USA.

Dr. Innes is a consummate learner whose passion is to help others become their best by utilizing their full potential and positively impacting their world.

www.ingramcontent.com/pod-product-compliance
Lightning Source LLC
Chambersburg PA
CBHW030910080526
44589CB00010B/236